SURVIVING RETIREMENT

FINDING PURPOSE AND FULFILLMENT
BEYOND THE BADGE

MEDINA BAUMGART, PSYD, ABPP

CONTENTS

DEDICATION

This book is dedicated to my husband, Tony. I could not have done this without you and your relentless support and encouragement. Thank you for your service as a police officer. Thank you for sharing your story and the lessons learned in hopes of easing the retirement adjustment for other police retirees. I will forever admire your tenacity, integrity, and character. You make me a better human, and I look forward to our future adventures and shenanigans. I love you.

ACKNOWLEDGMENTS

To those law enforcement retirees who have shared their stories with me over the years, thank you. I appreciate your courage and candor. I am forever humbled by your service and sacrifice.

FOREWORD

STEPHANIE M. CONN, PHD

Those that serve others with a strong conviction of their "why" are tireless in their mission. Medina is one of those servants. Medina's passion for supporting first responders is fortified by her love of her own first responder, her husband. I met Medina years ago as she was pursuing information to better help first responders retire well. Instantly, we connected over our mutual goal of supporting first responders who deserved better. We both recognized that the psychological impact of retirement had been overshadowed by the almost solitary focus on financial aspects.

As a former police officer, wife, and daughter of police officers, I wish that the guidance of this book had been available to my father. He served for almost forty years as a police officer and, four months before his death, wept as he spoke of his regret for his prioritization of work over family. At the end of his life, he knew that he could not change anything other than to express that he wished he had a do-over. I am profoundly sad for my dad and any other public servant who served without due regard for their own well-being and the relationships in their lives. I truly believe that Medina's guidance can save others from these heartbreaking conversations. This book would have been helpful for the officers I interviewed in my research about postponing retirement. Many had not mentally prepared, believing that retirement would mean a shift from "hero to zero" as they didn't know their value as a person and knew no other way to measure it than their work in first responder service.

As a treating clinician specializing in resilience, I found Medina's insights into how cops' nervous systems change over their careers to be a significant strength of the book. Too often, retirement discussions are limited to financial, psychological, and relational changes. While these are important, the physical changes influence your overall well-being and relationships. We have known the impact of chronic traumas on the nervous system for years and have historically taken the approach that it can't be helped. Medina counters this myth with straightforward guidance on rewiring a nervous system that has been conditioned for its conditions (policing) and not for the rest of their lives (home life, retirement life, family life, etc.).

In this book and, for that matter, in her training of others, Medina's familiarity with the culture is only surpassed by her commitment to supporting this population. Medina interweaves her professional and personal understanding of the issues facing law enforcement. In reading this, I felt like I was sitting with a person who had been there, done that, and understood it well enough to explain it simply (no psychobabble!). Medina's vulnerability in sharing her personal struggles with her husband's retirement is a gift to the readers as it relays the universality of retirement challenges. I believe this will allow you to recognize that you are not alone, that others have gone before you, stumbled, and got up.

Medina provides a balanced view of retirement- the good, the bad, and the ugly. She goes beyond that to equip you with tools to shift out of the bad and ugly while recognizing that your experience is quite normal for the retirement transition. Each chapter offers activities to both better understand and help yourself be well in retirement. The activities are worth their weight in gold! If you reflect on the inventories and make adaptive changes, you will be significantly more resilient. After all, resilient cops are those that treat resilience like officer safety in that you can only manage the risks that you are aware of. Each chapter is a call to action for you to increase your awareness and manage your risks. While this book is applicable to retiring police officers, family members will also benefit from reading this. You're going through the retirement transition as well.

I truly believe this book will equip cops and their families to proactively prepare for retirement and, for those already there, to build their resilience and enjoy life after policing. You deserve it!

Stephanie M. Conn, PhD
Licensed Psychologist, First Responder Psychology
Author of *Increasing Resilience in Police and Emergency Personnel: Strengthening Your Mental Armor*

INTRODUCTION

Toward the end of his law enforcement career, my husband was as crusty as they come. It was like he stepped off a page directly from Dr. Kevin Gilmartin's *Emotional Survival for Law Enforcement* book...everyone was an asshole, and everything was bullshit. By this time, he was on multiple blood pressure medications and was drinking alcohol regularly to help him stay sane. It saddened me to watch my husband, who absolutely *loved* being a cop, come home so angry and frustrated each day. As with many cops throughout their careers, he had become disillusioned and jaded. His last five years of being a cop felt different. The job had changed. Everything was more political. He felt like actually getting the job done was a constant battle with the powers-that-be, who would rather have him do less to avoid upsetting anyone or causing them problems. His career was winding down, and he was miserable.

I remember the day he called me from work. He had

twenty-nine years on the job, and his pension would max in just under twelve months. He asked, "Should I turn in my retirement paperwork now or stay one more year for the extra money?" Without hesitation, I responded, "Turn in the damn paperwork!" I could hear it in his voice that he was still contemplating it, but he turned it in. I later explained to him that I was worried he would have a stroke or a heart attack if he worked another year. Admittedly, I also wanted him to retire because I was tired of the spillover of work crap into our relationship. I was tired of his anger. I was done with his daily ranting. I was scared that the stress he was experiencing toward the end of his career would literally kill him.

When it came time for my husband to retire, we both naively believed the grass would be greener on the other side. Anything was better than him going to work and coming home pissed off every day. The psychologist part of me was nervous because I knew that my husband over-invested in his identity as a police officer and literally gave his blood, sweat, and tears to the job throughout his career. How would he cope with no longer being a cop? What would he do in his life after law enforcement?

As it turned out, we both vastly underestimated how *we* would adjust to him being retired. He struggled with no longer being a cop. I struggled with the new routine and helping him navigate everything he was experiencing. Regardless of the professional tools and training I had, I felt helpless and powerless to help him ease the pain he was feeling. We fumbled through it as best as possible and experienced some exceptionally difficult and challenging times.

The day after he retired, my husband felt immense relief from the stress he experienced toward the end of his career. After a few months, he was hit with a tidal wave of unpleasant emotions and thoughts. He experienced significant feelings of loss in retirement. He was no longer a police officer, and the camaraderie, mission, purpose, and routine that he was used to for so many years was suddenly gone. He felt lost as he tried to find his footing in civilian life. To cope with his discomfort, he leaned on alcohol and isolated himself. We argued more than we did when he was working. We both felt confused and frustrated. Retirement was supposed to feel better than this. The first year was tough, and it took him nearly two years to get used to being retired.

As he was settling into retired life, I handed my husband a notepad and asked him to write down everything he wanted to share with other police officers who were approaching retirement. His notes served as the foundation for me to learn more about how cops adjusted to retirement - both those who had an easy transition and those who struggled. I was also curious about how other spouses adjusted to their LEOs being retired.

My professional work with law enforcement officers predominantly includes counseling, consultation, and training. As I further explored the topic of retirement, I spoke with numerous law enforcement retirees and spouses. The adjustment process varied - some transitioned seamlessly while others experienced great difficulty making sense of their life after a career in law enforcement. I began to notice trends between the cops, spouses who adjusted well, and those who experienced difficulties.

Although there was some variation among retirees, those who struggled seemed to have some things in common. My husband's story and our relationship struggles as he adjusted to retirement were not unique. Others had similar experiences but often suffered in silence with little guidance and support.

I wrote this book in hopes of providing you with a roadmap of what to expect. Each chapter has a "Take Inventory" section designed to enhance your awareness of strengths and weaknesses in areas that are known to impact the quality of retirement for law enforcement retirees. I recommend using a notepad or journal to write down and keep track of your responses as you read this book. This information will help guide you toward actionable steps that you can take to reinforce your strengths and train up any areas that could potentially compromise your retirement well-being.

It is generally acknowledged that police work poses challenges to a well-adjusted retired life compared to other professions. This book is a collection of research-based information and experiential insights that my husband and I wish we had when preparing for and going into his retirement. We hope that sharing our story normalizes what you might experience. The reality is that not everyone will struggle, and you won't really know what to expect until you get there. You can, however, prepare yourself by training up for retirement in an effort to ease your adjustment and buffer against any residual trauma, stressors, or lifestyle changes that you may experience. Increasing your knowledge about what to expect will provide you with a broader frame of reference to interpret these experiences and make sense of them as you settle into life after your law enforcement career. If you are in a relationship, share this book with your partner because they are a key part of helping you adapt to retirement and will likely go through their own adjustment as you both get used to you being retired.

CHAPTER 1
UNDERSTANDING RETIREMENT

I attended a retirement seminar with my husband about one year before he pulled the plug. We both listened intently about the different aspects of financial planning and health benefits to consider in retirement. By the time the seminar ended, my husband and I felt better informed about how to prepare for his retirement. To be entirely honest, neither of us considered much of anything else about retirement beyond the information covered during that seminar.

It felt like forever for my husband to reach retirement age. As his retirement date approached, we both felt excited, nervous, and uncertain about what came next. As a police psychologist and his wife, I knew about the impact of law enforcement work on officers' well-being and had concerns about how my husband would adjust to retired life. We were both aware of the grim statistics on the average lifespan of cops *after* they retired and had already heard stories of this unfortunate reality. Despite everything we learned about finances and healthcare at his retirement seminar, none of that information prepared us for what came next.

THE HUMAN SIDE OF RETIREMENT

Although finances and health benefits are important components of retirement, traditional seminars tend to neglect the human aspects of acclimating to civilian life after a law enforcement career. What about the impact of the lifestyle changes inherent in retirement? What about the impact of these changes on spouses and families? Many law enforcement retirees have shared with me that they suddenly had to learn new ways of living that were vastly different from the life and job they dedicated themselves to for so many years. These abrupt changes were often accompanied by little preparation and few tools to ease the adjustment process for the retired officer and their family.

As a living and breathing human being, chances are that you will experience moments of discomfort or uncertainty as you approach and settle into retirement. *Many of these experiences are normal and temporary.* Some police retirees I've talked with share concerns that they might somehow appear weak or defective to peers or loved ones if they experience anything other than happiness in retired life. In my conversations with countless retired cops and spouses, several have shared challenges they experienced as they approached and moved into retirement.

What about the cumulative impact of police work? Despite its sometimes unpredictable nature, the job provides structure and standard operating procedures to guide you on what to do in different situations. Retired life lacks the structure you are used to, with no operating procedures to reference as you try to find your footing. Additionally, policing takes a toll on your mind, body, and relationships throughout your career. This cumulative impact does not just magically resolve itself when you retire.

One last general comment on the human side of retirement. You already know that the job trains your mind and body to *protect* themselves as a means of officer safety. Your training, coupled with your experience, have shaped your perspective about people and the world in general. It is normal to be skeptical or downright distrusting of the motives of others, scan your environment even when off duty, and sit with your back to the wall at a restaurant. This mindset and its accompanying behaviors become an automatic part of your daily life over the course of your law enforcement career. It is important to recognize that this protective stance runs counter to living well in retirement, which involves *connecting* with others and with a new mission and purpose.

Although retirement affects everyone differently, studies have identified certain factors that impact physical and psychological well-being in retirement. Aspects of your identity and personality, how you adapt to change, the quality of your relationships, the context of your retirement, and what you are retiring into can all impact how well you adjust to being retired[1]. Keep in mind that it is difficult to connect with anyone or anything when your armor is on. It takes time to learn to be less suspicious of people and to meet new people in retirement since these are contrary to everything your training and experience have taught you. It is important to know that protection and connection wire your body and brain differently. Successfully adapting to retired life typically involves shifting your perspective so that you can begin connecting with and experiencing the *good* things that life has to offer.

DO I STAY OR DO I GO?

Police officers decide to retire for various reasons, including reaching the coveted 30-year career milestone, experiencing prolonged job stress or dissatisfaction, or pursuing new opportunities that better align with their needs and professional goals. Some cops find it easy to make the decision to retire. Others struggle with retiring from a profession they have dedicated so much of their life to. Among those who struggle, common concerns include living a life without police work, lacking the security and comfort of a career, or having financial goals or burdens that make it necessary to stay on the job.

There are also situations in which officers are forced to retire because of administrative issues, discipline, organizational politics, or serious illness or injury. When retiring on someone else's terms, it is normal to experience feelings of anxiety, fear, worry, depression, and anger that compound the natural emotions and experiences that occur as one adjusts to retirement. There can be additional psychological pressure due to the discrepancy between how someone wanted to end their career versus the reality of how it actually is. Numerous studies also demonstrate that people who retire before wanting to do so tend to experience decreased psychological well-being as they enter retirement[2].

Whether you stay retired or seek post-retirement

employment, actively preparing for the impact of change contributes to your level of retirement satisfaction[3]. Law enforcement work is demanding and often results in some compromises to your health, hobbies and enjoyable activities, and relationships throughout your career. Although retirement is a major life transition, it also provides you with a positive opportunity to spend more time enhancing these areas.

YOU'RE A CIVILIAN...NOW WHAT?

Law enforcement work is unique in a variety of ways. You undergo rigorous training and experience things that most humans rarely, if ever, experience in their lifetime. The job demands so much that it is normal to become significantly invested in being a police officer at some point during your career. When it is all said and done, the reality is that the retirement process itself ultimately comes down to paperwork and procedures. Months prior, you submit the initial paperwork to retire. In the days leading up to retirement, you clean out your locker and desk and turn in your gear. On the day you retire, you relinquish your badge and your firearm and sign on the dotted line. Congratulations. You are no longer a sworn peace officer. Welcome to the civilian world. Now what?

Research on retirement for police officers further supports that the process of retiring can feel isolating[4]. Law enforcement retirees have shared with me that they were disheartened by the retirement process. They did not have grand ideas of the red carpet being rolled out, but they expected some expression of gratitude or appreciation that highlighted their years of service and sacrifice.

Instead of feeling the pride that many cops feel when they wear their badge as sworn police officers, these retirees expressed feeling tossed aside and insignificant, especially those who were off work IOD for some time prior to retiring.

The nature of policing inherently taxes your mental, emotional, and physical resources, both on and off duty. The extent to which this occurs contributes to how law enforcement retirees cope with the abrupt end of their careers when they retire. Think about the extensive training you undergo to prepare for becoming a police officer and the ongoing training throughout your career to hone and maintain your skills. How much training do you undergo to prepare for the abrupt transition from sworn peace officer to private citizen? When I ask this question to cops nearing retirement and those already retired, the answer that I hear in abundance is, "not much."

Take Inventory:
The Impact of Law Enforcement Work

Take a moment to think about your ideal retired life. Does where you stand today meet your expectations for retirement? Although some aspects of life are inevitably beyond your control, you still have the ability to actively restructure your post-retirement life and seek out the tools and resources needed to help you find purpose and fulfillment beyond the badge.

Actively preparing for change is a crucial component of achieving a well-adjusted life after your law enforcement career. It helps to begin by taking inventory of how your law enforcement career has impacted you over the years. This is important to help you identify the areas that might pose challenges to your well-being in retirement and will also help you manage some of your expectations for retirement.

As you answer the following questions[5], think about whether these changes have been positive or negative for you and how this might impact your well-being in retirement. I strongly encourage you to write down your responses. Awareness precedes change. Take however long you need to answer these questions. It is crucial that you are honest and thoughtful in your responses.

- How have your relationships changed? How about your family life? How about your friendships?
- Are you satisfied with your intimate relationship? How is your communication? Any resentments or other issues? If you are not in a relationship, what are some of the barriers to finding and sustaining a meaningful romantic relationship?
- What are your priorities in life (family, work, faith, health, leisure, friendships, intimate relationship, finances, hobbies, etc.)?
- Do you still do things you enjoy? What hobbies and interests do you have? Which ones have you abandoned?
- Do you find that your outlook has changed? How so? Is there evidence of mistrust, cynicism, or negative thinking?

- Do you often feel stressed? What are your signs of being stressed? Do you have difficulty relaxing?
- How well do you feel you are coping with stresses and strains from the job and from your personal life? What do you do when you notice you are becoming overstressed? How do you alleviate stress?
- How do you deal with uncomfortable thoughts, emotions, or memories? Do you ever feel overwhelmed by them? Do you engage in any avoidance or distraction activities?

If you have a spouse or significant other, I recommend that they also answer these questions about the changes they have experienced over the course of your relationship and law enforcement career. It can be helpful to share your responses with one another so that you can identify individual and relationship strengths and challenges. Use this information to work *together* to enhance yourselves and your relationship leading up to and into retirement.

PHASES OF RETIREMENT

Adjusting to retirement is a lot like getting used to being a cop at the start of your career. When you graduate from the academy, it is expected that you will use your training and knowledge to be good and effective at your job. Truth is, despite successfully completing the academy, you are still green and feel like you don't really know what you are doing. It takes some time on the job, learning via experience and training, and good mentorship to help you find your footing as you settle into being a cop.

Retirement is a similar process. You are presumed to have a good retirement after a career that literally taxes your health, sanity, and relationships. Not to mention the abrupt separation from a support network of partners whom your life literally depended on. It is normal to feel a bit out of place at the start of retirement. What you expect can vastly differ from what occurs as you settle into civilian life. Some retirees figure it out relatively easily, while others struggle to find their footing. Learning via experience, self-education, leaning on supportive loved ones, and talking with other retirees who can mentor you through retirement can ease your transition from public servant to private citizen.

A significant component of successfully navigating retired life involves making sense of being retired, which includes finding new purpose and meaning. Dr. Riley Moynes, a lifelong educator, struggled to make sense of how he was feeling in retirement and made it his mission to figure it out. Through his own experience and research involving interviews with hundreds of retirees, he identified four distinct phases of retirement that everyone generally experiences.

My personal and professional experiences working with law enforcement retirees have reinforced that this framework is helpful to enhance the understanding of the psychological and emotional adjustments that inevitably occur in retirement. Although each person is unique in how they move through these phases, this four-phase framework[6] highlights the general aspects of what to expect.

Phase 1: Vacation - This phase is exactly what it sounds like. You wake up when you want and do what you want each day. For most people, the vacation phase represents an idealistic view of retirement... relaxation and fun in the sun.

Phase 2: Feeling Loss and Lost - As the vacation phase loses its luster, you begin to feel a bit bored and miss the routine. Buckle up and get ready. This phase is often characterized by asking yourself, "Is this really all there is to retirement?" Significant losses associated with retirement begin to surface in this phase - routine, identity, relationships, sense of purpose, and, for some, a loss of power. You may also come face-to-face with divorce, depression, and/or physical and mental decline. You may feel like you have been hit with a lot all at once, which can be overwhelming. It is normal to experience feelings of fear, anxiety, and depression in this phase. Your existing supportive resources and how you cope with what you experience during this phase can make all the difference in moving you forward or keeping you stuck.

Phase 3: Trial and Error - As you work through phase two, you begin to ask yourself, "How can I make my life meaningful again?" or "How can I contribute?" The simple answer is to do the things you love and to do them really well. Unfortunately, this often involves some experimentation and trying new things. This process can sometimes deliver disappointment and failure, both of which are entirely normal in this phase. The goal here is to find different activities that will make you want to get up each day. Although this may very well push you out of your comfort zone, stick with it. If not, you risk slipping back into phase two and again feeling like you got hit by the proverbial emotional and psychological bus.

Phase 4: Reinvent and Rewire - Not everyone gets to this phase, but those who do are the happiest in retirement. This phase involves answering some tough questions such as, "What's the purpose here?" and "What's my mission?" In this phase, you are successful in finding activities that are meaningful and give you a sense of accomplishment. Almost always, this involves service to others. As you reinvent and rewire yourself, the losses in phase two are recovered.

THE BOTTOM LINE

Preparing for retirement involves more than financial planning and understanding your healthcare benefits. You are a human being behind that badge, and you have worked years in a profession that places unique demands on your physical health, mental health, and relationships. Much of the training and experience you have acquired on the job has shaped your mindset and behaviors to utilize a protective stance that is counter to living well in retirement. Finding fulfillment and purpose beyond the badge involves venturing outside your comfort zone to find the things and relationships that give your life meaning in your life after law enforcement.

Generally speaking, retirement is a four-phase process of change that involves different emotional, psychological, and lifestyle adjustments. Here is the bottom line...enjoy your vacation in phase one; be prepared for the losses in phase two; experiment and try as many new different things as you can in phase three; and squeeze all the juice out of retirement in phase four.

Adjusting to retirement is a process that varies greatly among officers and their spouses. Despite some of the individual factors that can contribute to how well you cope with the changes inherent in retirement, existing research reinforces that pre-retirement health and functioning matter. The first step in actively preparing for retirement is to take inventory across the areas known to impact law enforcement retirees. By responding to the questions in this chapter, you have already started this process. Hang onto your responses to reference throughout this book. In the following chapters, you will learn more about the specific areas that are important to achieve a well-adjusted retirement after your law enforcement career. If you find that you are doing well in a particular area, keep it up! If you find that you may struggle in certain areas, use the tools provided in that chapter to help you train up for a fulfilling life after your career in law enforcement.

CHAPTER 2
I GAVE YOU MY LIFE, AND YOU HANDED ME A RECEIPT

My husband was a cop's cop. He began his career at age 21, and by the time he retired, he literally spent more of his life as a cop than he did as a private citizen. He enjoyed police work and loved taking bad guys to jail. He was more than happy to work countless hours to get the job done. Weekends and holidays didn't exist in our household in the traditional sense. Police work took priority most of the time because it was what he loved doing. By the middle of his career, the vast majority of his close friends were cops and he had no interests or hobbies outside of law enforcement. He gradually lost interest in spending time with his non-cop friends because they "didn't get it." Being a cop was all my husband knew, both on and off duty. I think that is a big reason he struggled toward the end of his career and in the first few years of retirement. If he couldn't be a cop anymore, who the hell was he?

The retirement process within my husband's department further set the tone. I'm not quite sure what we both expected his last day of work to be like, but it definitely was *not* what happened. He cleaned out his desk and packed up all of his personal belongings. He turned in his vehicle and gear and obtained a receipt from his supervisor that confirmed all of his work property was received. He then signed the form that stated he was retiring and no longer had peace officer powers. There he was, standing in the office with a box of his personal belongings. He was no longer a cop. Unfortunately, nobody thought to ask if he needed a ride home. I was stuck at work and couldn't pick him up. Thankfully, one of his partners was able to bring him home. In my eyes, his agency failed him that day.

My husband said that he felt like he got fired on his final day at work. In almost an instant, he went from being an experienced cop who was respected by his peers to an outsider. All of the hours he put into the job. All of the criminals he took to jail. The two shootings and numerous other critical incidents he experienced. He sacrificed so much to be the best cop he could be. On his final day of work, it seemed like it was all for nothing. He felt discarded, isolated, and demoralized. When I asked him how he was doing, he responded, "I gave them my life, and they handed me a receipt." All I could do was hug him when I came home that day. He was hurting and still in shock and disbelief that he no longer had the career and police officer status he had embraced so proudly for most of his adult life. It broke my heart to see him like this, and I felt powerless to take his pain away. How could the very job he gave so much to not give a shit about him?

This experience got me thinking about the role that law enforcement agencies play in either enhancing or diminishing their officers' transition to retirement. In my professional experience working with end-career and retired cops, I have seen both sides of the spectrum. Some had great leaders and partners who physically and emotionally supported them through the retirement process. Others walked that process alone, which seemed to contribute to their feelings of isolation, loss, and demoralization. Although agencies and leaders can set the tone for how an officer feels going into retirement, how much of the officer's identity is tied up in being a cop can significantly contribute to how they adapt to civilian life.

As with some retirees, from time to time my husband returned to his agency and unit of assignment to visit old friends and stay in touch. He quickly learned how fast things change and how fast he was forgotten. Over the course of just a couple of years, he went from reconnecting with old partners over lunch to seeing new faces he didn't recognize and who looked at him like, *"Who is the old guy?"* He quickly went from being buzzed in at the front door on arrival to being asked who he was and waiting for someone to escort him inside. As more of his old partners and friends retired, he lost the camaraderie and felt no longer connected to a life that consumed the majority of his adulthood up to this point. This experience only intensified his feelings of isolation and reinforced the fact that he no longer belonged to the law enforcement family he knew for so many years.

POLICE OFFICER IDENTITY

Your professional identity as a police officer begins on day one of the academy. Throughout the academy, civilian characteristics are stigmatized and regarded as weak, naive, and unworthy of entering the law enforcement profession. Recruits are degraded when they display these lesser civilian attributes and idealized when they display police officer attributes[1]. If recruits successfully complete the academy, they have earned the esteemed status of police officer. If they fail, they are demoted to the lesser status of civilian. After all, not everyone has what it takes to be a cop.

After graduating from the academy, officers are thrust into a law enforcement culture that further promotes and reinforces embracing one's identity as a cop. You don't merely work as a police officer...you *are* a police officer. Over the course of your career, the long hours at work, shared experiences, and camaraderie can gradually erode other aspects of your identity. The camaraderie that develops during the formative years of your career reinforces that your new police family is who you rely on every day and the people your life *literally* depends on.

Depending on what age you were when you became a cop, you may very well have spent the majority of your life as a police officer by the time you retire. It can be easy for the job to overshadow your life outside work. Your old friends, hobbies, and interests may fade away because of necessity or simply because you are tired and don't have the time. This is one of the main reasons why healthy relationships with non-cops are so difficult to nurture and maintain over the course of a law enforcement career. Over time, these relationships may fade away as you notice it is difficult to sustain conversation or share interests with civilians who just don't get it. How others think and perceive the world may seem stupid or ridiculous.

It is common for certain law enforcement attributes to

spill over into your off-duty life over the course of your career. For example, always being armed when you leave your house, scanning the environment rather than enjoying yourself when out at a restaurant or social gathering, and maintaining a cynical outlook about other people and situations. If you have gradually lost interest in non-law enforcement activities or hobbies or feel unable to meet people or engage in conversation with non-cops, you may struggle a bit more in retirement compared to your peers who have been able to maintain other aspects of their identity over the course of their career. Look back at your responses to the "taking inventory" exercise in chapter one. Do you still do things you enjoy? Are there any hobbies, interests, or relationships that you have abandoned or neglected over time?

YOU ARE NOT YOUR JOB

Your personal and professional identities encompass the experiences, relationships, and values that influence your perception of yourself. This includes how unique you feel, the attitudes you have toward work and life, your goals and values, and your personality and character. Identity is important because it strongly influences your self-esteem, which impacts your feelings of self-worth and confidence.

Overidentification happens when a person identifies with their work in an excessive way and loses other aspects of who they are outside of their job. For some officers, work has become the most important thing in their life. Being a cop provides for their meaning, purpose, and sense of community. When thinking of the nature of police work and law enforcement culture, it is easy for officers to become consumed in their work identity over time. When you over-identify with your police officer role, you are likely to experience increased burnout, mental health issues, and challenges adjusting to retirement.

I've talked with many cops who believe that being "all about the job" is expected, celebrated, and rewarded. The demands of the job and law enforcement culture tend to normalize overworking. In some ways, overworking can actually feel comfortable. Although life can sometimes feel hectic and overwhelming, work offers some structure and predictability with its policies and procedures for what you need to do across different situations. For some, work can be an escape from the stress and challenges that life brings that don't have straightforward solutions. It is also common for officers to work in excess, even when not mandated, as a way to distract themselves from unpleasant experiences and numb their emotions.

IDENTITY AND RETIREMENT

When you lose your status as a police officer (as happens in retirement), it is normal to feel a bit lost and without a clear sense of purpose. If your identity is spread across different areas you value in life, you will better adapt to change in retirement because you have things that are meaningful to you beyond police work. If your personal identity is closely tied to your professional identity of being a cop, retirement can be a difficult and stressful experience. Think about it...why would you want to be less of who you are?

If you have overinvested in your police officer identity, retirement may spark the onset of a sort of personal crisis related to who you are, what you value, and your self-worth. Among pre-retirement factors that influence retirement well-being, identity matters[2]. For those who have overinvested in their police officer identity, retirement is likely to be perceived as a negative event with an emphasis on losses. For those who have managed to maintain an identity that is spread across other life roles, retirement is likely to be perceived as a positive event with an emphasis on gains.

Take Inventory:
Overinvested or Healthy?

Take a moment to examine your identity and the areas of life that you value[3]. Write down your responses. The below prompts and questions will give you a sense of how expanded your identity is (or isn't). If you are overinvested at work, your responses will guide the steps you can take to broaden your identity. The goal is for your identity to encompass areas of life that you value outside of law enforcement.

- **Step 1: Think about the areas of your life that you value.** Write these down. Some examples include health, family, work, spirituality / faith, friendships, education, community, intimate relationships, hobbies, and leisure activities. If you struggle with this, I'd like you to think about your ideal life and what that would entail. Or you can think about someone you look up to as having the ideal life outside of work…what areas of life do they seem to have that you would like to achieve?

- **Step 2: Think about how much you have been doing in service of each of these life areas.** Are there any discrepancies? For example, let's say you value friendships but haven't really spent the time connecting (or reconnecting) with friends outside of work. Or perhaps you value your physical health but have not been exercising or maintaining a healthy diet. Or maybe you have an interest in woodworking or another hobby but have not taken any steps to pursue it.

- **Step 3: Are you overinvested or underinvested?** Take a look at what you value and your actions in service of those areas. Are your actions overinvested, underinvested, or congruent with the life areas that are important to you? It can help to draw 3 columns on a piece of paper and sort your valued life areas based on if you are doing just right, too much, or too little in each of those areas.

- **Step 4: Align your actions with your valued life areas so that you can expand your identity within each of these roles.** Time to get to work! Look at your responses to Step 3. For each of the life areas you are underinvested in, identify and write down at least one thing you can do to invest in this area. For each life area you are overinvested in, identify at least one or two things you can reduce and re-allocate time and energy into another area that is underinvested, or that aligns well with the things you value. The goal is to shift your efforts toward establishing and maintaining a diverse identity that is well-balanced across multiple life areas that you value.

TRAIN UP FOR RETIREMENT

When you retire, your identity as a police officer abruptly ends. If you have no other interests beyond being a cop, the loss of the job can enhance the loss of meaning and purpose. If your identity expands to other areas of life you value beyond being a cop, you are likely to have an easier time finding purpose and fulfillment beyond the badge.

Broadening your identity beyond work helps to buffer against the stressors associated with law enforcement work and the inherent toll it takes on your mind, body, and relationships over the course of your career. An expanded identity positively influences your mental health by offering purpose and meaning, increasing self-esteem, and providing a greater sense of control over your life[4]. As you work on expanding your identity and strengthening other roles outside of law enforcement, it helps to set weekly goals. How you choose to work on expanding your identity is flexible and can be adjusted throughout your career and into retirement. The goal is to achieve a life that is consistent with the things you value so that you can foster meaning and purpose in life during and after the job.

CHAPTER 3
FEELING LOSS AND LOST

When my husband first retired, it felt like ten thousand pounds of stress lifted from his shoulders. His blood pressure went down, and he lost some of the stress weight. He was no longer angry all the time, and he was smiling and laughing more. I took some time off work when he retired. It felt like we were both on vacation, and it was great. My husband was happy that he survived his career. I was happy that both he *and* our relationship survived it. The sense of relief that came with him retiring was like the exhale you take after a long hard day. *It's over now. He made it. We made it.*

After years of hard work as a police officer, my husband mostly wanted to sit around and do nothing right after he retired. I completely understood this and was happy to let him indulge himself. He spent so many years in one of the most physically and psychologically demanding and taxing professions. He deserved to kick his feet up and take it easy. My husband would often enjoy a drink and a cigar in our backyard during the week, and we would spend the weekends watching movies and enjoying time with each other. Our weekends were *actually* our weekends. No more work phone ringing at all hours. No more being called into work. It felt like he was on vacation.

The start of my husband's retirement was a great few months. It felt like he was on vacation and we had zero stress. As he settled into this vacation phase of retirement, things gradually lost their luster. This is when the reality of retirement hit him (and us) like a ton of bricks. My husband started feeling the impact of no work routine and having nothing to do. He felt like a fish out of water in civilian life. He thought to himself, "Is this really it?" As a cop, he had a clear mission and purpose each day. Although the job can be unpredictable, he felt a sense of competence in his ability to handle whatever came up. He lacked meaning and purpose in this new chapter of life. Over time, he experienced profound feelings of loss about what his life used to be like and felt uncertain about what life is going to look like in retirement.

My husband missed being a police officer and the camaraderie. He missed putting bad guys in jail. He missed the adrenaline. Despite being grumpy during his last few years on the job, he missed going to work. He missed feeling connected with his partners, the job, and a purpose. My husband was a cop for so many years... now what? He was bored and struggling to make sense of life after law enforcement. He had no hobbies, no interests, and no meaningful friendships outside of law enforcement. Shortly after the vacation phase of retirement ended, my husband sought a full-time civilian job in an effort to keep busy. He quickly realized that he no longer wanted to wake up to an alarm or to be told what to do. He also had little patience for administrative stressors and supervisors. Ultimately, he went back into retirement after a few months of post-retirement employment.

NEW ROUTINE

Law enforcement work is demanding. Establishing and maintaining a routine throughout your career helps things feel less chaotic and keeps things predictable (for you and your family). Just as you adapted a routine based on the demands of the job, you will need to adapt a new routine to meet the demands of retirement. Some law enforcement retirees welcome this change with open arms, and others find it a bit scary or overwhelming. This change can be so impactful that some officers choose not to retire or delay their retirement because they fear boredom or not knowing how they will pass the time.

When your usual routine abruptly changes in retirement, it is normal to feel a bit awkward or lost as you figure out what your new routine will look like. Individual experiences vary, but there are some common responses among law enforcement retirees when it comes to the lack of routine in retirement:

- *Behavioral* - increased alcohol consumption, increased food intake, difficulty sitting still
- *Physical* - headaches, sensation of being "keyed up," sleep difficulty, appetite and weight changes

- *Emotional/Psychological* - boredom, loss of purpose, moodiness, depression, anxiety, irritability, feeling a sense of urgency
- *Relational* - isolation, increased conflict

Take a minute to look back at your responses to the questions in the "Take Inventory" section in the last chapter. If your personal identity is strongly tied to your professional identity as a police officer, you may experience intensified feelings of loss and lack of purpose early on in retirement. As you work to broaden your identity in areas outside of law enforcement, think about some of the things you can do in retirement. Keep in mind that how quickly you develop a new routine and how you cope with these changes contributes to you making forward progress through the phases of retirement, moving backward, or getting stuck.

SOCIALIZATION

Camaraderie is at the heart of law enforcement culture. The loss of your police family and the strong bonds you have with your partners is another significant change experienced in retirement. Fostering new and *healthy* connections with people can help you bounce back from this loss. It may not be the same as when you were a cop. The goal here is not to replace your law enforcement family. To be honest, I think that is irreplaceable.

Socialization is an important component of a well-adjusted retirement. I understand that, for some of you, interacting with people may not be on your top ten list of enjoyable activities. It is okay to be selective and to keep your social circle small; however, it is also important to venture out a bit and meet people outside of the law enforcement world. Hear me out. As a cop, you encounter the worst that life has to offer. You are trained to maintain an attitude of distrust toward others as a means of officer safety. Your experience on the job reinforces that people can't be trusted and that people are capable of doing bad things. All of this helps your brain reinforce the idea that people suck. If you limit socialization in retirement, your brain will continue using this connection, and you will likely experience increased feelings of social isolation, ongoing cynicism, and depression. If you meet other people in retirement, you are giving yourself the opportunity to learn new things…to keep your brain sharp. You may even find some new interests or hobbies because of the new people you meet.

In order to nurture and maintain social connections, it is essential that you step out of your comfort zone a bit. Your brain needs to learn that not everyone is out to get you or is untrustworthy. Each social interaction you have that doesn't end in the worst-case scenario is an opportunity for your brain to establish a new connection and reinforce a healthier perspective that not all people suck. You can still maintain a skeptical attitude about the intentions of people, but it is important to balance distrust and protection with trust and connection. Social connections are built into our biology, and positive interactions release feel-good chemicals which reinforce connection and counter isolation and depression.

MENTAL STIMULATION

As a police officer, your brain and body get used to operating under a certain amount of stress and mental stimulation on a regular basis. You are exposed to prolonged periods of hypervigilance, stress hormones, and sleep deprivation. You experience increased job demands, politics in the workplace, and administrative stressors. Life as a police officer is often filled with lots of multitasking, split-second decision-making, problem-solving, and managing complex and challenging situations. Although the nature of the stress and mental stimulation you experience on the job changes as you go to a new assignment or move up the ranks, your mind is constantly processing a wide range of stimuli to inform your decisions and actions.

When you retire, both your brain and your body have to abruptly learn how to operate under different conditions. The private citizen life is not always filled with the same levels of mental stimulation and excitement as cop life. I'll discuss this more in chapter five. For the time being, simply recognize that this change in stress and mental stimulation can further contribute to how you adapt to the change in your daily routine. As you adjust to this change, it is normal to feel bored, restless, fidgety, or have difficulty powering down.

Take Inventory:
Activities Outside Law Enforcement

If you haven't already done so, begin exploring activities outside of law enforcement work. If you are uncertain what to do, that is okay (and you are not alone). Start experimenting with different things and talk with peers for some additional ideas. Try to focus on things that keep you active, not sedentary. Be sure to include exercise and a healthy diet, as these are both known to improve mood, increase energy and motivation, decrease stress, and improve cardiovascular health.

Using the below prompts, start planning your new routine. It is a good idea to write down your responses so that you can begin to map out your retirement routine.

- **Step 1: Identify five enjoyable activities you can do in retirement**. Think of things that you used to do or have always wanted to do but never had the time. Find something that interests you or that you want to learn more about. Talk with your peers and any retirees you know for some suggestions. Using your responses from last chapter's "take inventory" activity, be sure to identify activities that encompass areas of life that you value outside law enforcement.
- **Step 2: Identify at least one or two activities that you can do over the next month.** Be practical and choose activities that fit into your existing life demands. The goal is to begin incorporating enjoyable activities pre-retirement to build a foundation that you can expand on when retired.
- **Step 3: Schedule time to spend on these activities.** Be specific and intentional with this step. If you are unable to spend time on an

activity, what gets in the way? How are you going to address this barrier? Changing your routine means addressing your habits. Were you genuinely unable to work on an activity, or do you need to prioritize things differently?

If you struggle to identify some activities outside of law enforcement, here are some examples of activities that retirees have shared with me. It is okay if some of these don't appeal to you. I encourage you to find at least one or two activities that you would be willing to try. It can also help to talk with retirees you know to get a sense of what their new routine looks like.

- *Exercise* - walk/hike outdoors, go to the gym, ride a bicycle, go swimming, go scuba diving, stretching exercises daily to maintain flexibility
- *Diet* - cook new food recipes, take a cooking or nutrition class, try a new restaurant
- *Mental Stimulation* - play an instrument, read a book, learn woodworking or a new hobby, take a class on a subject that interests you, work on puzzles, organize your garage/home, learn to do home repairs, go to a museum
- *Relaxation* - get a massage, sit outdoors and listen to relaxing music, yoga or meditation
- *Socialization* - go camping, volunteer, spend time with family, connect with a friend

It is normal to feel awkward or uncomfortable as you try something new. Keep in mind that it is okay to feel moments of frustration and disappointment as you try new things. It may take a few tries before you start feeling comfortable enough to begin enjoying new activities. Stick with it until you have at least a handful of activities outside law enforcement work that you enjoy.

TRAIN UP FOR RETIREMENT

Actively restructuring your lifestyle in retirement is essential and often involves some trial and error. It is important to be intentional and specific when working toward a new routine. Avoid relying on general statements such as, "I'll have plenty to do when I retire" or "I'll figure it out when I get there." Start rewiring your brain and body to new activities and habits. As you incorporate activities outside law enforcement, choose things that keep you active and mentally stimulated, activities that involve some degree of socialization, and also some activities to help you relax and wind down.

One piece of feedback I often get from retirees is that they sometimes find their schedules busier in retirement than when they were working. As you work on some activities to incorporate into your new routine, it is important not to overschedule yourself so that you are constantly staying busy. This could inadvertently delay the onset of any emotional or psychological reactions if you are staying active as a means of emotional avoidance or distraction. It is important to balance staying active with periods of relaxation so that your body and mind learn to shift between these states.

At least one year prior to retirement, start practicing being retired. If you are able, take additional time off – perhaps an extra day connected with your RDOs or a week off every other month. If your Department does not pay out certain leave time you have accumulated throughout your career, use those hours to take some extra days off. The point here is to get your brain and body used to a reduction in the level of work activity it is used to and to begin engaging in activities or hobbies you might do in retirement.

It is also helpful to reduce or eliminate paid overtime to get used to the financial constraints of a retirement pension. If you are struggling with meeting life demands on what you will make in retirement, take a look at your finances and meet with a financial planner if you need help with restructuring your monthly budget and spending. If you are working overtime to pay down debt or save up for retirement, be sure that your financial goals are clear and that you have a budget in place that aligns with your retirement income.

If you seek post-retirement employment, I recommend spending at least 6 months in retirement prior to doing so to give your brain and body some time to adjust to being retired. If possible, work part-time and choose something outside the law enforcement profession. Some retirees choose to continue utilizing their skills to consult, teach, or work in law enforcement or a related field. If you do so, be mindful of social circles and attitudes that reinforce some of the negative byproducts of law enforcement work (more about this in chapter five).

CHAPTER 4
PHYSICAL WEAR AND TEAR

My husband started his career like all street cops, in patrol. He eventually moved to the detective bureau, where he worked robbery and homicide cases until moving to street narcotics, vice, and gangs. He eventually moved to a major narcotics team and spent the last half of his career working various task forces and assignments, including surveillance teams and clandestine lab teams. Some of his lab work was before protective equipment became standard practice. By the end of his career, he had developed what I call the "Law Enforcement Package" of health issues - high blood pressure, high cholesterol, diabetes, acid reflux, sleep apnea, back issues, and numbness down his leg when he stood up for longer than a few minutes.

As my husband approached his retirement, he began to experience significant anxiety and worry about his health. He was not alone in having health issues by the time he retired; nonetheless, he finished his career physically better off than many of his partners who had been diagnosed with cancer or suffered from a heart attack or stroke. He unfortunately also had friends who died before they retired or shortly after their retirement. He was convinced that it was just a matter of time before he had a heart attack or was diagnosed with cancer. He just hoped to make it to retirement first.

A couple of years before my husband's retirement, he scheduled numerous doctor appointments and underwent several medical tests to assess, diagnose, and treat his health issues. He was prescribed multiple medications and told by his doctor to stop drinking alcohol, eat healthy, and exercise more. He took his medications daily, but the doctor's lifestyle change recommendations were a bit more difficult to maintain consistently.

After retirement and some fumbling to figure out his new routine, my husband began eating healthier and exercising regularly. He lost weight and was able to stop taking some of his medications. He was the healthiest he had been in years. He felt good and was motivated to maintain his healthier lifestyle. He was adamant that he would *not* become the statistic of retired police officers who die within five years of retiring.

As my husband approached that five-year mark in retirement, his anxiety and worry about his health re-emerged. He had lost more friends to heart attack, stroke, and cancer by this time. This increased his concerns that he would eventually be diagnosed with a major illness or disease or have a heart attack or stroke just before or just after he reached that five-year goal. Fortunately, that did not happen, but his concerns highlighted the very real physical health risks that law enforcement officers endure throughout their careers.

THE PHYSICAL IMPACT OF POLICE WORK

Law enforcement work is physically demanding, with the general assumption that all officers will encounter some form of injury, illness, or disease while on the job that they may carry into retirement. Daily activities such as standing for long periods of time, repeatedly getting in and out of your vehicle, and wearing pounds of gear gradually take a toll on your body. Additional risks for physical injury resulting from physical altercations, foot pursuits, defensive tactics training, and exposure to excessive noise levels all contribute to the physical health issues experienced by police officers.

Compared to other occupations, police officers have higher morbidity and mortality rates, predominantly due to cardiovascular disease and cancer[1]. The years of biological ups and downs, adrenaline and cortisol production, shift work, and sleep deprivation all contribute to increased rates of obesity and hypertension among cops[2]. Additional exposure to chemical and biological hazards further contributes to elevated cancer risks for police officers compared to the general population.

INJURIES, CHRONIC PAIN, AND SERIOUS ILLNESS

If you are dealing with chronic pain, injuries, or serious illness, you may experience additional challenges that impact your quality of life in retirement. Research has demonstrated a correlation between serious medical illness, chronic pain, and psychological/emotional distress, including:

- Decreased energy and motivation
- Social isolation
- Loss of purpose
- Feeling helpless, powerless, or hopeless
- Anxiety, depression, or anger
- Sleep disturbance
- Relationship problems

Certain medical conditions involve taking pain medication or other habit-forming medications that can place you at risk for developing substance abuse issues. It is possible for physical pain and emotional pain to merge over time, resulting in added psychological dependence on these substances to ease emotional distress. Increased alcohol consumption is also common as it may enhance the effects of pain medication, numb pain, or help you fall asleep (despite the significant effects of alcohol on your quality of sleep and your body's healing processes). Alcohol and many prescription pain medications often have a cross-tolerance, meaning that you require more of both substances to feel the desired effects. Prolonged use of these substances can result in additional issues such as cognitive and memory problems, cardiovascular issues, sleep disturbance, anxiety, depression, and relationship problems.

THE ELUSIVE GOOD NIGHT OF SLEEP

When was the last time you had a good night of sleep? How about a full week of good sleep? As a police officer, sleeping well can be challenging and, at times, next to impossible. Factors such as shift work, stress, elevated levels of cortisol, traumatic events, and personal and work demands contribute to sleep difficulties among cops. Sleep deprivation is problematic for your physical health and general well-being, both on the job and in retirement. The consequences of poor sleep are well-researched and have been associated with increased alcohol use and increased risks for injury and serious disease[3]. Unfortunately, the nature of police work poses some unique challenges to getting a good night of sleep.

Policing is a 24/7 job, and shift work impacts officers at some point during their law enforcement careers. Your body has its own sleep-wake cycle that is influenced by light and dark, as well as natural chemical changes that help to wake you up and make you sleepy. Shift work inherently alters this natural sleep-wake cycle, especially when working overnight shifts or extended hours. Essentially, you are working against the body's natural processes. Even when changing shifts to working days, it can take months or years for the body to readjust. For some officers and retirees, their body never fully readjusts.

An overactive mind is another common issue among officers who experience sleep difficulty. In fact, sleep research has shown that the brains of people with insomnia are overactive in areas where they should be less active when falling asleep. This can be due to the brain simply being unable to turn off or being preoccupied with stress and worry.

Here is the bottom line: your body and brain heal and restore themselves when you sleep. Although police work can pose challenges to getting a good night of sleep, there are still some things you can do to promote sleep. The

"Train Up" section toward the end of this chapter offers some additional suggestions.

ROUTINE MEDICAL CHECK-UPS

Dealing with health issues or being in poor physical health in retirement can cause additional strain on your emotional and psychological well-being. You may be able to mitigate the impact of certain health issues by simply staying on top of your physical health through annual medical check-ups. Often, police officers avoid these routine medical check-ups because they feel they are "too busy" or worry that they may find out they have a medical issue. Many cops don't want to hear from their medical provider that they need to eat healthier, avoid alcohol, exercise more, or stop smoking.

Here is the reality…if you are having physical health issues, avoiding it won't make it go away. The earlier you know about a health issue, the sooner you can start formulating a treatment plan to address the issue. In many cases, simple lifestyle modifications to exercise and nutrition is all that is needed. For more serious health issues, early detection and intervention often improves outcomes and extends your life.

One thing we know is certain…poor physical health in retirement diminishes your quality of life, and certain health issues can also impact your psychological health. Living well in retirement also involves taking control of your physical health. Although certain things may be beyond your control, there are still things you can do to maintain a healthy lifestyle leading up to and into retirement.

Take Inventory

Spend a few minutes answering the following questions to assess your physical health and any existing issues or needs.

- Date of your last physical exam: _____.
- Do you have any known health concerns that have not been regularly followed up on?
- Do you have any health concerns that have not been mentioned to your doctor?
- How is your sleep? Do you have any issues getting to or staying asleep? Has someone mentioned that you snore loudly or stop breathing in your sleep? Do you wake with headaches or still feeling exhausted despite sleeping?
- If you are experiencing chronic pain, is it being managed effectively? If not, have you explored additional non-medication-based intervention options to supplement your current treatment regimen?
- What is your current exercise routine? How often do you exercise? What types of exercises do you do? Do any physical issues impact your ability to exercise?
- What does your current diet consist of? Have you talked with your doctor about which foods to increase or avoid for certain medical issues? Have you met with a dietician or nutritionist for

an individualized diet plan to meet your physical health needs and goals?

TRAIN UP FOR RETIREMENT

Take a look at your answers to the above questions. If you have any health concerns or have room for improvement with your diet and exercise routine, it is time to get to work. If you are in good health with an established diet and exercise routine that is working for you, keep it up! Below are some additional recommendations to help you maximize your quality of life when it comes to your physical health in retirement.

If it has been more than one year since your last annual physical exam, or if you have existing concerns or issues that have not been addressed, schedule an appointment with your medical provider. If your current provider is not listening to you or adequately addressing your needs, find another medical provider in your network. If you struggle with proper exercise and nutrition, consider seeking additional support and consultation from a professional trainer, dietician, or nutritionist.

If you are dealing with chronic pain, injuries, or serious illness in retirement, it is important to have a good network of both emotional and tangible support. In addition to traditional medical interventions to manage discomfort related to medical issues, individual counseling can teach you additional skills to help you further manage your pain, process thoughts and emotions related to pain and medical issues and provide additional coping tools. Support groups can also be beneficial to gain additional information and support (refer to this workbook's resources section for some recommendations). If you are being treated through the workers' compensation system, make sure to ask how retirement will impact your medical treatment. For example, your coverage options and availability of workers' comp providers may change if you move out of state. Be sure to seek out this information beforehand, if possible, to avoid additional stress and frustration when dealing with the workers' comp system to receive medical treatment in retirement.

If you are not sleeping well, talk with your medical provider to obtain any additional tests to rule in or rule out underlying health issues that might be impacting your sleep. The next step is to develop a pre-sleep routine to relax your body and prime it for sleep. Allow yourself around one hour to wind down before bedtime. Activities such as listening to calm music, stretching, doing relaxation breathing exercises, and drinking a cup of non-caffeinated tea or warm milk can help. Give yourself at least 30 minutes of gadget-free time and dim the lights to help you transition to sleep. Keep your room around 67 degrees for optimal body cooling. Non-stimulating sounds such as white noise, running a fan, or soothing nature sounds can also help you fall asleep faster. It is also a good idea to limit alcohol, tobacco, and caffeine six hours before bedtime. Avoid eating large meals three hours before bedtime. If you are hungry, try a light snack 45 minutes before bedtime. Melatonin supplements can help with sleepiness but avoid using it regularly because it can interfere with the body's natural ability to produce melatonin. Recommended dosages for melatonin are 5mg for women and 10mg for men. Avoid combining sleep aids which can actually disrupt the quality of your sleep and make you feel drowsy or hungover upon waking.

If an overactive mind is interfering with sleep, here are a couple of tools that can help, in addition to establishing a pre-sleep routine:

Constructive worry. Bedtime is the least appropriate time to worry because the anxiety it creates will keep you awake. One way to combat worry at bedtime is to schedule "worry time" during the day. This may sound counterintuitive, but it actually helps you gain control over intrusive worry and rumination. During this time (10-30 minutes is typically sufficient), your task is to write down any concerns you have that may cause you to worry or keep you up at night. Draw two columns on a piece of paper - label one "concerns" and the other "solutions." For each concern, write down any actionable steps you can take to address or solve the issue. If taking action is not feasible, write down things you can do to reduce or alleviate the associated emotional discomfort. If you are unsure what to do, write down any additional information you need to help guide any actions you take, whether task-oriented or emotion-focused.

Change your perspective. Your thoughts can impact your sleep. Sleep-interfering thoughts tend to focus on worry or stressful or traumatic events. Examples of sleep-promoting thoughts include: "One night of poor sleep is not the end of the world," "Nightmares are disturbing but not real, and I'm safe now," "This feeling will pass," or "My body is reacting to a memory, and I am safe right now."

Relaxed body, quiet mind. The body and brain like to be on the same page. For example, when you experience unpleasant emotions, your body tenses up, and your stress response is activated. Likewise, it is difficult to sustain a quiet mind at bedtime when the body is stressed out. Learning to relax your body promotes sleep. Common techniques include relaxation breathing, progressive muscle relaxation, guided imagery, body scan, and meditation.

Maintaining good physical health on the job and in retirement is an ever-evolving process that requires ongoing self-assessment and modifications. Police work is physically demanding, and it is crucial to stay informed and active in your efforts to counter the health conse-quences associated with a law enforcement career. Try some of the above tools and activities to maximize your health and general well-being in retirement.

CHAPTER 5
CHANGING GEARS

T he job often followed my husband home. For many years, his work phone would ring 24/7 because of the nature of his work assignment, so it never actually felt like he was off-duty. Whether he was on the phone, talking with partners, or at home, he had two modes. He was all on or all off.

When he was "ON," he was irritable, keyed up, scanning the environment, and unable to sit still. This was even more apparent when we would run errands or go places when he was off-duty. As his wife, I noticed this would often shift my mood to feeling anxious, stressed, or irritable. An "ON" husband and an anxious or irritable wife were not the best combo for our relationship. This was a stark contrast from his "OFF" mode, which was when he finally crashed. This would look like he was disengaged, disinterested, and zoned out. He would often have the television on but wouldn't pay attention or would be mindlessly scrolling through social media or playing games on his phone. This would shift my mood toward frustration and eventual disengagement. Needless to say, this took a toll on him and our relationship.

Toward the end of his career, my husband was increasingly crusty and had significant difficulty powering down when home. He was jaded and angry. His work perspective of dealing with bullshit and people being assholes or idiots (sometimes both) had completely infiltrated his off-duty life. His brain was locked on this jaded perspective, and his body was stuck in the "ON" position.

As he settled into retirement, he experienced fluctuations in his mood and activity level. He was fidgety and couldn't sit still while simultaneously not having stuff to do. This also meant he was irritable. When he was irritable with nothing to do, he would tend to find stuff to be angry at or start arguments with me over little things. Eventually, he would crash, at which point he was relegated to the couch and zoned out. During this "OFF" period, he experienced some fatigue and lack of motivation, as well as feeling a bit down and depressed. He often isolated himself, and it felt like he was disengaged from our relationship. From my perspective, it was clear that his body and mind were having a hard time transitioning to being retired, much like he had difficulty transitioning from work to home when he was on the job.

TRANSITIONING FROM WORK TO HOME

Law enforcement work is stressful to the body and mind, even on a good day. A certain amount of stress is needed for you to perform optimally and maintain the necessary hypervigilance on duty to keep you safe. However, as you acclimate to stress over time, your perspective shifts and you become essentially mentally numb to the sensation of stress while your body continues to physiologically experience it. The persistent nature of stress in law enforcement work accumulates over time and can impair your mental and emotional clarity, mental and emotional health, the quality of your relationships, and your physical health.

At some point in your career, you have probably heard someone say, "Don't bring the job home." In theory, this sounds like a great idea. As a living and breathing human being, it can be a bit more complicated than that. Cops endure a myriad of stressors that challenge their well-being and can make the transition from work to home life a difficult task. The residual gunk from the workday can have serious consequences on your physical health, mental health, and relationships if you don't effectively transition your brain and body after your shift.

HYPERVIGILANCE: MORE THAN A MINDSET

Cops are trained to maintain hypervigilance as a means of officer safety. You are constantly scanning your environment for potential threats and keeping yourself at the ready should you need to take action. Many officers talk about hypervigilance as a mindset - almost as if you need to have the mental will and fortitude to remain hypervigilant. Although I can appreciate this perspective, it negates the fact that hypervigilance is actually a biological process that has a tremendous impact on the human body.

Hypervigilance places your body in a heightened state

of arousal. This is the biological state that allows you to maintain a threat-based perspective – a crucial component of officer safety. While hypervigilant, your limbic system and prefrontal cortex are engaged in a complex process. In other words, the part of your brain associated with emotion and the body's stress response is interacting with the part of your brain where decisions are made. This complex biological process allows your brain to make quick assessments and decisions to guide how you respond to the variable situations that you encounter. Over the course of a law enforcement career, this takes a toll on your brain and body and can significantly impact your physical and mental health and the quality of your relationships.

When on duty, hypervigilance feels exciting and stimulating. It can be energizing and help to enhance your focus and performance. The body's natural response to this heightened state is to slow things down and recover. Unfortunately, you don't have the luxury of allowing your body to rest and recover when on duty because this could compromise your safety and seriously impact your performance and decision-making. This is why stimulants such as caffeine, nicotine, and energy drinks are popular among police officers. These substances help your body maintain the hypervigilance needed to stay safe and get the job done.

When off-duty, your body needs to recover from its prolonged state of hypervigilance. Just as hypervigilance is a biological process, so is the recovery period. During this time, the prefrontal cortex goes offline. This means that the decision-making center of your brain, along with its functions that assist with attention, judgment, and impulse control, essentially cease to function appropriately. It generally takes 18 to 24 hours for the body to recover from the biological effects of hypervigilance. This can make it challenging for officers to recover fully between shifts since they are often back at work. Those who are off work may take a full day to feel normal again or spend time drinking caffeine to keep them awake while they try to engage with their family or run errands.

NOT EVERYONE IS AN ASSHOLE

As cops, you are trained to approach people and situations with a general attitude of distrust until proven otherwise. This allows you to maintain the hypervigilance needed to help keep you safe on the job. Makes sense. Now consider the impact of approaching people and situations in this manner, repeatedly...countless times...for years.

This generally distrustful attitude toward human nature and motive is reinforced by the calls you respond to and the things you encounter as a cop. When dealing with the criminal element, cops are exposed to dangerous situations and often see the depravity of what human beings are capable of doing to one another. There is also the added impact of the nationwide increases in violent crimes, assaults on officers, relaxed legal consequences for criminal behavior, and anti-police sentiment in political, media, and social media outlets. The cumulative impact of these events can reinforce the notion that people are bad and cannot be trusted. So... does that mean you are cynical?

I've heard officers say, "I'm not cynical, I'm skeptical." Although both cynics and skeptics can doubt the intentions of people, there are some key differences. A skeptical person is also open-minded and open to evidence to the contrary. A cynical person will almost always choose to doubt and disbelieve or discredit someone or something despite evidence to the contrary.

So, how does someone become a cynical person? Cops aren't born that way. Adopting a cynical attitude is something that happens over time for a variety of reasons. Here are some key factors that influence cynicism. I'd like you to think about how your own experiences, both on the job and in your personal life, might impact whether cynicism develops and to what extent.

- *Worldviews and predictions about life* – these come from situations and events that we see in-person, on social media, news stories, etc.
- *Personal defense mechanism* – this is when a person prevents themselves from being open to love, friendships, etc. because they cannot trust someone for fear of being hurt
- *Adverse or traumatic life event(s)* – these experiences can cause a person to "close up" emotionally and relationally to protect oneself
- *Poor stress management or burnout* – this can impact how well our rational brain is working and whether our emotional brain hijacks how we respond

If left unchecked, a cynical attitude can negatively impact your overall well-being and destroy both personal and work relationships. When combined with prolonged hypervigilance, cynicism results in officers becoming "salty" or "crusty" over their careers. As discussed in chapter three, socialization in retirement is a vital component of successfully navigating civilian life. This does not mean that you need to be a social butterfly. You just need to form a few meaningful social connections with others. That is difficult to accomplish when your cynical attitude keeps people at a distance.

Take Inventory:
Changing Gears

Take a few minutes to answer the following questions to get a better sense of your ability to transition from work mode to being off-duty.

- What is your current routine when coming off shift? Do you change out before going home? Do you intentionally spend time to begin transitioning to being off-duty before you get home?
- How do you spend your time driving home? Do you listen to music, mentally process the day, zone out, or talk on the phone?
- Do you feel that you have changed gears from on-duty to off-duty by the time you get home? If not, how long does it generally take you to feel that you have been able to change gears?
- What do you come home to? Do you have a significant other, kids, roommates, or other

family members that demand your time and
attention?

- What have you tried to do to help your body
and mind change gears after work? Has
anything been helpful?
- Have any of your friends or family members
commented that you always bring work home
or that you are too uptight, irritable, or "short-
fused" when home? How about being
disengaged, zoned out, or disinterested?

DOWNSHIFTING

The typical pattern of hypervigilance looks like a bouncing
ball. Your body goes up, then down, then up again, then
down again, then up...you get the point. If you don't do
anything to intervene with the bouncing ball, it eventually
bottoms out and stays there. The longer your body fluctu-
ates in these extremes, the bigger the toll it takes on your
health and relationships.

Rather than crashing at the end of your workday, you
can do some things to help your body ease the biological
transition and maximize your recovery period. This will
also help you re-engage your life and relationships when
off-duty.

The concept of downshifting refers to reducing the
intensity of something. Think about how your brain and
body operate when on duty. If you were a car, your
tachometer would be in the red. However, unlike a car
engine, your brain and body cannot recover by simply
turning off at the end of your shift. You can, however, shift

into a lower gear to help your brain and body slow down and recover.

Downshifting is an intentional process that cannot be scrolled away on social media, played away on video games, watched away on television, or drank away with booze. If you notice that you are doing these things or finding it necessary to keep busy off-duty, you may be engaging in emotional avoidance or distraction activities. While this can provide you with some short-term relief from your workday, the long-term consequences on your physical health, mental health, and relationships can significantly impact your quality of life.

Over the course of your law enforcement career, you adapt to the biological changes related to hypervigilance and mental stimulation associated with police work. Think of it like going to the gym. Your brain and body exercise the muscles required to sustain these job demands. As the muscles get stronger over time, the weight gets easier to lift. If these work-mode muscles are the only ones exercised, the recovery muscles will atrophy. This means that you will tend to default to the two extremes of hypervigilance and disengagement. This generally results in health issues and relationship problems over time. The goal of downshifting after work is to help exercise the recovery muscles so that your brain and body are balanced between being at work and being at home.

When you retire, your routine changes. You no longer need to maintain hypervigilance as a means of officer safety because you are no longer on duty. This does not mean that you stop paying attention. It just means that your body and brain take some time to adjust. This can result in fluctuating mood (anxiety, irritability, and depression are common), a sensation of feeling "keyed up or unable to sit still," and increased arguments with loved ones due to an inability to effectively power down.

TRAIN UP FOR RETIREMENT

Begin training up for retirement by using some of the below techniques (or others) to help your body and mind downshift after work. Find at least one thing you can do prior to getting home and one thing you can do at home to help your body change gears. Consistency is essential. Be sure to exercise the off-duty (recovery) muscles to balance the effects of those well-exercised hypervigilance and cynicism muscles that are reinforced when you are on duty. If you work an assignment that requires you to be on-call or answer your phone after hours, it is especially important that you put forth an effort to help your brain and body recover a bit before (and between) the phone rings.

Dressing Down. As you dress down after shift, begin to slow your brain and body by grounding your senses. Start by focusing your attention on your physical senses. As you remove pounds of gear and your ballistic vest, take a few seconds to enjoy how much lighter your body feels. As you get out of your uniform, notice how the fabric feels, the texture of the buttons, and the temperature changes (warmer or cooler). If you wear something other than your work uniform, the process is the same for each layer of clothing that you remove. If your brain starts thinking about the workday or things you need to do after work, mentally place your mind on pause, take a breath, and redirect your focus to your physical senses. This takes time, but with regular practice, you can train your brain and body to slow down and start recovering from your shift.

Take it and Leave it. Find a coin or token of some kind that fits in the pocket of your work uniform. Take it with you, and put it in a designated spot when you change out at work or when you get home. As you do this, imagine that you are placing work on pause to be picked up the next workday when it is put back into your pocket.

Systems Check. When you get in your car to leave work, take a minute to scan your internal systems. How is your breathing? Any physical tension or discomfort? Take a couple of minutes to focus on your breathing and slow it down with a steady inhale-exhale pace. Each time you exhale, imagine a little bit of that stress or discomfort leaving your body. As you drive home, focus on slow and steady breathing at each red light or stop sign. Before you exit your vehicle, take another minute or two of slow and steady breathing to exhale more of the residual stress or tension from your workday.

Brain Dump. Unload your workday by taking ten minutes to literally dump whatever is on your brain – thoughts, emotions, or anything else – on a piece of paper. Don't worry about forming coherent sentences or censoring what you write. The point here is to make some room for off-duty life by releasing some residual mental gunk from your workday. You can do this when you get into your car before you drive home or shortly after getting home. When you are done, shred it or tear it into pieces and throw it away. As you get rid of it, imagine that you've disposed of some of that mental engine gunk so you can function better.

Limit work stuff off-duty. Pay attention to how much

time you spend talking about work when you are on your own time. It is a good idea to reduce how much time you spend re-hashing the workday when you are off-duty. Although it can feel like you are just venting or telling war stories, this can inadvertently keep your brain and body in work mode when you are off the clock.

CHAPTER 6
I'M FINE

As my husband approached his retirement date, he began to reflect on his law enforcement career. He would recount the good times and the more difficult stuff. This time around, it was more than just telling war stories. He was *feeling* emotions that he had compartmentalized throughout his career. From my husband's perspective, he did not know what the hell was going on. He felt unable to control his emotions and would occasionally have difficulty holding back tears for seemingly innocuous things like a movie or a news story.

Throughout his career, he was generally well-contained when it came to talking about or showing more vulnerable emotions. As he neared retirement, it was like his brain was finally getting a chance to process the cumulative emotional impact of his law enforcement experience. He was feeling very normal emotions but had some difficulty navigating that experience because he was accustomed to being "fine."

I'M FINE

When police officers are asked how they are doing after a tough call, the overwhelming response is, "I'm fine." When it comes to *feeling* emotions, law enforcement culture trains you to "suck it up" and "lock it down." This is important and necessary for officer safety when responding to difficult situations. We know that emotions can cloud judgment and decision-making, both of which are important qualities to possess as a police officer. Nonetheless, cops are human beings, not robots.

Compartmentalizing emotion is a skill learned in the academy and reinforced throughout your career. Some police officers also learn to internalize and/or avoid emotions from personal experiences in their life, such as their childhood upbringing or in response to traumatic events. It is important to know that effectively compartmentalizing emotion on the job does *not* mean that you are not impacted.

The job trains you to compartmentalize emotions but not how to engage your emotions when needed. *How* you feel things and what you do with those feelings is often not talked about amongst officers because of the stigma associated with being perceived as "weak" or unfit for the job. The reality is that unprocessed emotions will come up eventually, often in ways or at times that are not entirely convenient. Some may attempt to cope with this reality by chronically avoiding emotional discomfort by keeping busy, distracting themselves, drinking alcohol, or using other substances.

EMOTIONAL AVOIDANCE: FUNCTIONAL OR DYSFUNCTIONAL?

Think about how you have coped with chronic stressors and uncomfortable emotions or situations throughout your career. Dark humor and sarcasm are common ways to lessen the psychological impact of traumatic or stressful events. They defuse the discomfort and tension of an uncomfortable situation. Among cops, drinking alcohol is another culturally appropriate way to quiet the mind and numb the emotional burden of a bad call or tough day at work. Distraction is another technique to keep the brain busy. A quiet mind can be a scary place for officers because they know what is lurking just behind this thin veil of emotional avoidance. Although these coping behaviors can seem effective at the moment, is emotional avoidance healthy or dysfunctional?

Over time, coping with stress and discomfort via emotional avoidance and distraction provides increasingly shorter-term benefits and longer-term costs at the expense of your mental, emotional, and relationship well-being. This inhibits your ability to tolerate emotional discomfort, which can make you feel easily overwhelmed or create the need to constantly keep busy, which can make it difficult to power down. This places your body and mind in chronic survival mode, which prevents you from actually engaging in the things you enjoy doing. Although emotional avoidance can help you deal with the imme-diate discomfort, these emotions typically come back or resurface in other ways. For example, someone may feel the need to constantly stay busy to avoid feeling, experi-ence frequent irritability or anger and lash out at family, or completely disengage from themselves and their loved ones. If this sounds familiar to you, is this something that you want to continue doing in retirement?

MISMANAGED STRESS

As a police officer, you are trained to operate under stress. Over the course of your career, your mind and body will habituate to both the physical and mental aspects of stress. This helps you manage stress on the job and can be beneficial to performance when experienced at optimal levels. However, this also shifts your perspective of what constitutes something stressful or what it feels like to be "stressed out." As a result, your ability to tune into stress micro-signals diminishes, and it becomes difficult to recognize when your body and mind are stressed and need to recover. This can lead to mismanaged stress spilling into other facets of life – poor judgment and decision-making at work or home, irritability or having a short fuse, unhealthy communication, and engaging in unhealthy coping behaviors. You may also stop caring or blame others for your misfortunes.

Working in a law enforcement environment can further condition your brain to focus on things that are wrong or problematic. This is a helpful mechanism when there are physical safety issues, as you can often use this information to drive actions in service of safety. This brain mechanism is less helpful when perceiving threats to your internal/emotional safety that result in you feeling helpless, powerless and/or out of control. When stress is not managed effectively, the brain can adopt a sort of "emotional tunnel vision" and stay locked on negative thinking, which can increase perceived stress and decrease effective problem-solving. Doing this in retirement can be detrimental to your well-being and can also make it difficult for you to nurture healthy relationships or enjoy time off duty.

WARNING SIGNS

Chronic mismanaged stress coupled with emotional avoidance can contribute to burnout and compromise your mental health. Officers and retirees can get stuck in a stressful state and become discouraged or frustrated when their usual way of coping is not working. Here are some warning signs:

Activity level changes. Watch for significant sleep disturbance lasting more than one week. This might be sleeping too much or not enough. You may feel overly tired, unable to concentrate, and irritable. Take a look at your daily activity level as well; social isolation or acting impulsively or taking unnecessary risks can also be warning signs.

Interpersonal difficulties. Pay attention if you are "short" in conversation or are experiencing more arguments or disagreements with people. You may also hear from someone else that you are not your usual self, grumpier or angrier than usual. Alternatively, you may shut down and avoid human interaction altogether at work and at home.

Work-related difficulties. Work performance issues (tardiness, frequent callouts, forgetting equipment, report writing difficulties, etc.), decreased performance and/or high error rate, increased conflict or disengagement from co-workers, or impaired decision-making and judgment

Substance use. Drinking or using substances to feel better or to not feel at all is problematic. Engaging in behaviors such as driving under the influence or carrying your firearm when intoxicated are also problematic. Additionally, engaging in promiscuous sexual activity, spending excessively, and/or gambling as a means to feel better can also be signs of unhealthy coping.

Take Inventory:
Healthy or Avoiding?

In addition to the "Take Inventory" emotional coping questions you answered in chapter one, take a few minutes to thoughtfully answer these additional questions to gain further insight.

- What emotions are uncomfortable for you?
- What are your stress warning signs? How do you know when you are not adequately managing your stress?
- How do you currently cope with these unpleasant emotions? What do you do when you feel this way?
- What are some behaviors you engage in to avoid or distract from emotional discomfort?
- Do you feel afraid or anxious when you think about having to experience uncomfortable emotions?

TRAIN UP: STAYING ENGAGED

Cops do not run away from a physical threat — they engage it. That is the goal for dealing with uncomfortable emotions: Stay engaged and work *through* it. Emotions are signals that alert us to real or perceived threats in our internal or external environment. For example, fear and anxiety alert us to a threat that we may need to protect or prepare for, anger signals a threat and the need to fight, and sadness signals loss and the need for recovery. At times, uncomfortable emotions can trigger an avoidant or fearful response. Think about the last time you did something to avoid feeling uncomfortable emotions. What did you do? Was your emotional avoidance functional or dysfunctional?

Our emotions are meant to be felt. Although avoidance may seem helpful in the short term, it can actually worsen the intensity and duration of your discomfort as time goes on. Here are some tips to combat emotional avoidance and re-engage (or stay engaged) with your feelings:

- **Notice it and name it.** When something happens, take the time to check in with how you are feeling and name the feeling(s) — for example, happy, excited, anxious, sad, angry, disappointed, and/or hurt. No need to judge or understand it; just identify what it is and acknowledge that it is there.
- **Do an internal systems check.** Spend time tuning into your internal environment and focusing on the physical sensations associated with emotional discomfort. Often, particular feelings trigger a series of thoughts or stories about what the feeling means or says about us or others. When this happens, you are *thinking the feeling*. Instead, shift your focus to *feeling the feeling* in your body. Identify where you feel it in

your body. It can help to mentally scan from head to toe and just notice any areas of physical sensations in response to the emotions. Perhaps you notice that you have a clenched jaw, a lump in your throat, an increased heart rate, butterflies in your stomach, and so on. As you perform this internal systems check, pay attention to your breathing and try to breathe slowly and deeply. Continue to do so until the discomfort passes or becomes less intense.

- **Is it realistic or helpful?** Now that you have identified *what* you're feeling, examine whether it's realistic or helpful. For example, are your feelings exaggerated or appropriate for the situation? Is the feeling helpful for you? What need(s) is it signaling? What can you do that is healthy and productive to meet that need?

TRAIN UP FOR RETIREMENT

When we are stressed, we revert to what we know. This also goes for how you cope with unpleasant emotions, memories, or events. If you lack consistent training of healthy coping skills, you will likely revert to unhealthy ways of coping in retirement. It is normal for retirees to experience a re-emergence of unresolved emotions or memories once they retire. This can result in depression, anxiety, panic, emotional overwhelm, intrusive thoughts or images, guilt, anger, grief, and sleep disturbance. If inadequately managed, these symptoms can create signifi-cant distress and impact your well-being in retirement. Emotions are natural, but avoiding negative feelings can also feel natural. Rather than avoid or distract yourself from unpleasant emotions when off duty, I challenge you to stay engaged and ride the wave. Use the above tips or come up with something that works for you so that you're not spending unnecessary energy avoiding the feels.

CHAPTER 7
MENTAL AND EMOTIONAL IMPACT

A few months into retirement, my husband felt depressed. Much of the anger he experienced when he left his department had subsided (for the time being), and he crashed hard. He felt lost in civilian life and no longer had a sense of purpose. He got down on himself and second-guessed his decision to retire. From a logical perspective, he agreed that things were better without dealing with the bullshit of the job and the daily interactions with supervisors who seemed to prioritize politics over police work. He knew he was miserable by the time he retired, but he was also now dissatisfied with being retired. Despite being miserable at work, I think he felt like he still had a purpose as a police officer and was able to deal with all the assholes and bullshit because this was familiar territory for him (despite how unhealthy it was).

My husband missed the adrenaline and stress. He had invested so much in being a police officer and doing good police work throughout his career that it ultimately took over numerous aspects of his life. He wanted to be back in a world where he had a clear mission and purpose and where he felt a sense of accomplishment and confidence.

My husband recognized that he was depressed and no longer had the job to distract him. He felt like a fish out of water. How could he possibly make life meaningful again as a civilian? He made efforts to connect with his old partners and friends. He felt isolated in this new chapter of his life. He still lacked a routine at this point and struggled to find the motivation to get moving each day, let alone try something new. He wanted to feel the camaraderie and sense of belonging to something special.

About six months into retirement, police work began infiltrating daily life again (despite him being retired). He dreamt of work more often. He felt angry and irritable again. To cope with such unpleasant emotions and thoughts, he reverted to what he knew…alcohol. His drinking became excessive and reckless. The days of feeling like he was on vacation and enjoying a cigar and whiskey in the backyard were gone. He was bored and drinking every day. He sometimes felt overly emotional, and he didn't understand it. The lack of meaning and purpose, the loss and feeling lost, and feeling like a social outcast made him feel more emotionally distraught and out of control each day. He was struggling…heck, *we* were struggling.

CUMULATIVE IMPACT

The very nature of law enforcement work is taxing on your mental health, and it is normal to experience symptoms of depression, anxiety, and post-traumatic stress injuries at some point throughout your law enforcement career. I say this to normalize the impact that your work as a police officer has on your mental and emotional health. In addition to the repeated exposure to trauma, violence, and death that is typical throughout a law enforcement career, police culture reinforces some unhealthy coping habits (i.e., substance use and emotional avoidance) and stigmatizes vulnerability or help-seeking behaviors. It is important to note that symptoms do not mean disorder, and not all cops will develop a serious mental health issue. However, it is important to understand how the job can contribute to mental health issues that, if left untreated, will negatively impact the quality of your retired life.

The mental stimulation, hypervigilance, and stressors encountered on the job allow the brain to distract itself from the residual mental and emotional impact of policing. There is often not enough time to fully process what you encounter in a workday because you have to go to the next call or only have so many hours until you are back at work. This facilitates the compartmentalization of emotions that is required for officer safety. While working, this may seem like no big deal or a necessary part of the job. But there is more to it.

Unresolved issues that have developed over years of a law enforcement career can impact both your personal well-being and the quality of your relationships. If you do not prioritize your mental health, you may find it difficult to navigate any mental health symptoms or emotional discomfort you experience in retirement. Just like the body and brain must recover from the biological process of hypervigilance after a shift and over the course of your career, you also need to mentally and emotionally recover to maintain optimal mental health and functioning. What happens in retirement when your brain is no longer occupied by daily activity like it was when you were a cop?

Without the distractions of work, it is quite possible that your mind will wander to past incidents or unresolved emotions. This can feel uncomfortable, at best, and downright agonizing for some. I have talked with many retirees who experience symptoms of depression and post-traumatic stress injuries for the first time in retirement. When combined with the loss of their police family support system, retirees can feel even more isolated and distressed. In an effort to cope with these unpleasant emotions and experiences, retirees may lean on unhealthy habits that carried them through their law enforcement careers. If left untreated, these mental health symptoms can gradually spiral into issues that significantly impact functioning and, in extreme cases, lead to death by suicide.

DEPRESSION

Among cops I've talked to and worked with, depression tends to be viewed as a sign of mental defect or weakness when that is unequivocally false. Depression results from several factors, including the genes we inherit, thyroid and testosterone levels, medication side effects, shift work, sleep deprivation, and exposure to negative people and events[1]. Some of the treatment interventions and medications developed to treat depression aim to correct a chemical imbalance in the brain that influences thinking and mood. This means that depression isn't merely a state of mind...it's a *legitimate* medical issue. Some studies have shown that depression occurs at a higher rate among police officers than the general population. One large-scale study showed that 70 percent of police officers endorsed depressive symptoms[2].

When I talk about depression, I'm including both symptoms of depression and the clinical diagnosis of a depressive disorder. Although the magnitude of the symptoms and resulting functional impairment varies, depression involves changes to your thoughts, feelings, and behaviors. It is also common for depression to change how you view yourself, others, and the world. Think about what cops encounter in any given week…they see the worst that humanity has to offer. The mental and spiritual toll of police work can make officers lose their faith in people and the world. In addition to administrative and organizational stressors, this can negatively influence your thoughts and emotions to the extent that it interferes with your ability to function well and sustain meaningful, healthy relationships. Remember, this is just the impact of the job and doesn't include other non-cop life events that can contribute to depression, such as the loss of a loved one or dealing with serious health issues.

ANXIETY

Anxiety is another issue that exists among police officers. Like depression, a variety of factors contribute to anxiety, and there are biological changes that occur, such as a chemical imbalance and physical changes, including increased heart rate and respiration, sweating, tingling extremities, and others. Therefore, anxiety is also a *legitimate* medical issue influencing one's thoughts, feelings, and behaviors. It often involves worry and fear that encompass a wide range of concerns related to health, relationships, job demands, finances, or specific situations such as being in traffic, on an airplane, at a high elevation, etc. Among police officers I've worked with, anxiety seems to tap into themes of control, danger (real or perceived), and underestimating coping ability.

Control is paramount in police work and an essential component of officer safety. In the context of your job, control is acquired via verbal and physical means and through various tangible tools, policies, and procedures. Control is often challenged when confronted with the seemingly less tangible experience of emotional discomfort or situations that are beyond one's control, such as staffing shortages, schedules, shift work, administrative procedures, health issues, etc.

A sense of danger, real or perceived, can also contribute to feelings of anxiety and worry, especially when an officer feels that they are vulnerable to (emotional or physical) harm. Additionally, cops are trained to always consider the worst-case scenario and maintain hypervigilance (both of which can also contribute to anxiety). In situations where physical threats to safety exist, you are generally equipped with the training and tools needed to reduce and/or neutralize the threat. It gets a bit more complicated when emotional vulnerability or threats to emotional safety exist. When it comes to experiencing emotional discomfort, it can feel like you are not in control with no clearly identifiable "fix" to solve the issue.

An overestimation of danger and an underestimation of coping ability are distinct hallmarks of anxiety. This also contributes to feeling out of control and vulnerable. This is why treatment for anxiety generally involves equipping you with tangible tools to better regulate the physical responses that accompany anxiety (to enhance feeling in control) along with skills to balance thoughts that contribute to increasing or maintaining the anxiety.

POST-TRAUMATIC STRESS INJURIES

Post-traumatic stress injuries (PTSI) can occur following direct or indirect exposure to actual or threatened death, serious injury, sexual violence, and/or repeated exposure to aversive details of the traumatic event. Police officers encounter these types of incidents at an alarmingly higher rate than the general population. Additionally, officers are often back at work before fully processing the incident and recovering from the normal mental, emotional, and physical reactions that occur. This means that officers are exposed to additional traumatic events and are also unable to avoid places or situations that activate intrusive images, memories, thoughts, and mental replays or flashbacks associated with past events. This can contribute to our brain and body's normal healing processes becoming stuck. If unresolved or not adequately processed over time, these symptoms can cause significant distress and seriously impact functioning on and off duty. As with depression and anxiety, post-traumatic stress injuries can result in changes to our brain and body on a biological level, affirming that this is also a *legitimate* medical issue.

It is important to note that not all critical incidents will result in post-traumatic stress injuries. The *traumatic* component occurs when the interpretive framework that guides our expectations and actions has lost its capacity to organize the experience in a meaningful and manageable way[3]. Additionally, one's traumatic stress vulnerability is influenced by a variety of pre-and post-exposure factors, in addition to the factors of the critical incident itself. This is why officers experience different responses to the same incident and why some seemingly "bounce back" easier than others. This multi-factor understanding of post-traumatic stress injuries can also influence how a retiree experiences and recovers from any post-traumatic stress responses experienced in retirement.

You probably noticed that I referred to post-traumatic stress *injuries* rather than *disorder* terminology. Although formal diagnosis is an important component of informing treatment interventions, I believe that labeling something as a "disorder" implies some sort of personal defect or weakness. Saying that you have an injury implies that it can be healed. In my professional experience, this change in terminology can influence how law enforcement officers and retirees perceive their post-traumatic stress-related difficulties and how they approach treatment. If I go to my doctor for an injury, I expect that it can be healed to some degree, if not fully. If I go to my doctor for a disorder, my perspective changes and I feel like I am doomed to deal with this for the rest of my life (not super motivating for treatment). The good news is that a wealth of research on post-traumatic stress has demonstrated good outcomes with evidence-based treatment interventions for trauma.

IS THIS NORMAL?

When evaluating your symptoms as being normal versus problematic, the **B-FIIT**[4] acronym is a helpful metric. If you have any concerns, it is important to seek further consultation from a trained mental health professional to determine what additional steps are needed to help resolve any problematic symptoms.

- Any deviations from **Baseline**? Your baseline is your "normal" daily functioning, including mood, sleep, appetite, and other factors. It is common for your baseline to shift after a traumatic or stressful event. However, things should return to baseline in about a month.
- **Frequency**. How often do symptoms occur?
- **Intensity**. How vivid or strong are the symptoms?
- **Interference**. The degree to which the symptoms create problems in your functioning or become apparent to others (family, spouse, co-workers, etc.). Pay attention if others comment that you are "different" or "not your usual self."
- **Time**. How long have your symptoms been going on? How long do they last when they occur?

Take Inventory:
Mental Health

Take a few minutes to answer the following questions to assess potential mental health needs. If you answer yes to any of these questions, think about how this impacts you both currently and how it might impact you when you retire.

- Do you experience any issues that might be due to work-related exposure to a traumatic incident? *Common examples include intrusive or unwanted imagery or replay of incidents, sleep difficulty, avoidance of stimuli that remind you of the incident, extreme hypervigilance or feeling "keyed up," depression, anxiety, fearfulness, irritability, emotional numbing, or detachment.*
- Do you find yourself keeping busy to avoid thinking of disturbing events and/or avoid dealing with unpleasant emotions?
- Do you experience times when your emotions bubble over – for example, feeling a lump in your throat or becoming tearful for no apparent reason? Feeling angry or lashing out at others?
- Do you engage in unhealthy coping behaviors? *Examples include using alcohol or other substances to alleviate discomfort, engaging in addictive behaviors (e.g., gambling, spending, sex), isolating from others, and engaging in risk-taking or reckless behaviors to feel "a rush" or tempt fate.*
- Do you feel hopeless about yourself or your future? Have you ever thought about suicide or just not being around anymore?
- Have you lost someone or something and never fully processed or grieved that loss?
- Are there other issues in retirement that could create additional stress or strain on your quality of life? *Examples include caring for an ill family member, not having a support system to lean on, financial problems, chronic pain or serious illness, or forced retirement.*

RECOMMENDATIONS IF SEEKING MENTAL HEALTH TREATMENT

Law enforcement is a highly specialized field; therefore, treating cops is just as specialized. You want someone who understands your field. If you seek mental health treatment, do so from a *licensed* mental health provider. Depending on where you live, there may be too few or too many to choose from by simply conducting an online search or via private insurance providers. Unfortunately, many providers tout themselves as "specialized" in treating law enforcement, despite having little to no specialized training or experience working with law enforcement personnel. Therefore, it is important to do your homework and take the time to screen available mental health providers to help determine if they are a good fit for your treatment needs. Here are some questions to ask when screening a provider:

- How long have you been practicing as a licensed mental health provider?
- What is your experience working with law enforcement and other first responders? Approximately how many have you treated?
- What is your exposure to police culture?
- What is your philosophy and approach to helping? What is your therapy style?
- What kind of training and specialties do you have?
- What can I expect from doing counseling with you? What does a typical session look like?

- What is needed from me to make progress in counseling?

TRAIN UP FOR RETIREMENT

Begin training up for retirement by looking honestly at your responses to the questions about your mental health. What are your existing issues and concerns? What tools do you have to counter the negative impact of the job? How much time have you invested in taking care of your mental health throughout your career?

Make the commitment to prioritize your mental and emotional well-being so that you can live well in retirement. If you have the necessary tools and resources, begin using them! If you recognize the need for additional tools and resources, explore what is available to you. This includes formal and informal peer support, educational materials, books, podcasts, and organizations dedicated to serving the mental health needs of law enforcement personnel. If you decide to pursue mental health treatment, screen the provider using the above questions and bring your responses to the mental health questions and any other relevant concerns or questions to your initial appointment.

CHAPTER 8
RELATIONSHIPS

My husband's retirement impacted our relationship. He experienced the effects of significant changes to his daily habits and was struggling to function and find purpose and meaning beyond being a cop. As he navigated these challenges, consequently, our relationship experienced some growing pains. One of the biggest changes we experienced almost immediately into his retirement was an increase in arguments about insignificant things. As we fumbled through it, we realized that while I tried to help him with what he was experiencing, I was simultaneously experiencing a significant adjustment of my own.

As an LEO wife, I spent years adapting to his work schedule and developing my own daily routine. When he retired, my routine abruptly changed also. As much as I loved having him home where I knew he was safe and without the daily work, anger, and stress, I felt irritable and a bit overwhelmed. I vividly remember talking to him one day after weeks of trying to figure out why I was feeling this way. We sat on the couch, and I told him, "I love you so much, so please don't take this the wrong way, but...you are *always* here!" He paused, and then we both let out a sigh of relief along with a good chuckle. He understood exactly how I felt. The funny thing is that when he was working, and I was in school full-time, he felt the same way when he would walk through the door after a long workday. This was our "a-ha" moment and actually helped us understand one another. From that point on, we began working together to meet in the middle and figure out *our* new routine. By no means was it a perfect process, but we had a direction and a common goal.

Another challenge I experienced as a spouse was how to help my husband through what he was experiencing. As a psychologist, I have the necessary knowledge and tools to help other officers and their spouses through this same issue. As a wife, it was difficult to apply what I already knew because of my emotional connection to my husband. I felt like a mirror that fogs up. The knowledge and tools were there, but my emotions made it difficult to see clearly. I felt helpless and powerless as my husband experienced the grief and loss of such a huge part of his identity and camaraderie. I found myself wanting to fix it to take away his hurt. But he wasn't broken. What he experienced was *normal*. He just needed me there, as his wife, so he didn't have to work through it alone.

Over time, my husband and I worked together to help him establish a new routine, identify and engage in enjoyable activities, and navigate some of the ups and downs he experienced as his brain and body adjusted to being retired. From a relationship standpoint, we took things back to basics. We are two imperfect humans working together to be better versions of ourselves so that we could continue to grow our relationship. Throughout this process, communication was (and still is) key!

IMPACT OF POLICE WORK ON RELATIONSHIPS

Law enforcement work is tough on relationships. When you think about it, being a police officer inherently conflicts with being a spouse/parent/etc. As a cop, you need to keep your head on a swivel because someone may try to hurt you. This threat-based attitude of distrust is what keeps you safe. You also experience the ugly side of humanity, and you witness people's pain. All of this wires your brain and body for *protection*. In your personal relationships, you need to trust and *connect* with loved ones. It is almost like you are balancing two different worlds, often with little guidance on how to effectively do this in a healthy way. Many law enforcement couples and families struggle because they don't have the necessary tools to tune up their relationships over the years. Just as you evolve over the course of your law enforcement career, so do your personal relationships. Retirement is another chapter of your life that also impacts your spouse and family.

Throughout your career, your loved ones (especially those you live with) have developed a routine around your work. They learn to operate independently without you around much of the time because of your job demands. As you and your family shift from limited daily contact to being around each other 24/7…it takes some getting used to. During the adjustment period, it is normal to experience increased conflict with loved ones. Some retirees have even reported a desire to return to work as a means of alleviating relationship conflict. Whether you are actively doing things together or just co-existing in the home, retirement can involve some adjustment in how you interact with and relate to your significant other or family members. This can test your communication skills and the relationship itself.

Supportive, healthy relationships have been shown in numerous studies to buffer against stress and are a vital part of a well-adjusted retired life. It is important to talk with your spouse and loved ones ahead of time to come up with a plan to ease the retirement adjustment for everyone involved. It takes a village to get through a law enforcement career. The same applies in retirement.

COMMUNICATION PITFALLS

Communication is difficult to master in any relationship, let alone with the unique challenges of police work. At work, your communication with subjects is strategic, with an often-distrustful attitude towards the person as a means of officer safety. This is *very* different from the goal of communication with your loved ones—which is to connect, foster trust, and convey support. Different communication goals mean different communication strategies are needed.

Police officers are used to guiding conversation toward a specific goal. Any unnecessary information tends to be abruptly cut-off, and the subject is redirected to provide only what is necessary for the task at hand. Behaviors such as stumbling over words, talking around a subject, or providing extraneous information, are often viewed as indicators that the subject is lying or attempting to mislead you. The reality is that your loved ones may exhibit some of these communication behaviors *without* malicious intent. If you are interpreting your interactions with loved ones through work lenses, chances are that you will modify your tone and body language in a way that can intimidate or overwhelm loved ones. This can inadvertently create an unhealthy communication loop in which either or both of you shut down, become defensive, and / or become argumentative.

Multitasking while communicating with loved ones is a no-no. While you may be able to juggle several tasks on duty, the reality is that many of these things are on autopilot. Doing something repeatedly creates a habit. This means that our brains process the information differently than when we are intentionally concentrating on something new or different. Communicating with your loved ones is *not* a task-oriented activity...it's connection-oriented. Each interaction is an opportunity to connect, foster trust, feel heard and understood, and convey genuine care and concern. You cannot connect with someone while multitasking. Think about a time when you wanted to talk to someone while they were engaged in another task, such as watching television, typing an email, scrolling through their phone, and so on. What was the underlying message conveyed when they didn't make eye contact or stop what they were doing to listen?

THE PROBLEM-SOLVER

Cops are problem solvers by nature. While this may work for on-duty tasks and interactions, your loved ones are not problems that need to be solved. Often, they just need a sounding board. In some cases, the issue may not need solving; rather, it's just a simple need to work through what they are thinking and feeling to make sense of things. By jumping into problem-solving mode with a loved one, you might inadvertently invalidate and dismiss their feelings and/or their own ability to work through their problems. Taking on the problem-solver role in both personal and work relationships over time can contribute to feelings of burnout, emotional numbing, detachment, indecisiveness, fatigue, apathy, and resentment. If you haven't already seen it, check out the "It's Not About the Nail" video on YouTube. It's a humorous take on this topic.

Take Inventory:
Relationship Health

Reflect on the current status of your personal relationships, particularly those with your spouse or significant other and your family. In addition to the "Take Inventory" relationship questions you answered in chapter one, take a few minutes to thoughtfully answer these additional questions to gain further insight.

- Identify 3-5 strengths in your meaningful personal relationships. What do you like about each of these relationships? If you find this difficult to do, think back to a time when you were truly happy in these relationships. What about the relationship made you happy?

- Identify 3-5 challenges in these relationships. What don't you like?
- What are the behaviors that *you* can change to enhance these relationships? What are your communication strengths and pitfalls?
- If you are not in a romantic relationship, what are some of the barriers that prevent you from having one? Any lessons learned from past relationships?

GETTING THINGS BACK ON TRACK

Communication is a crucial component of healthy relationships, but we are not always functioning at our best. Good communication helps you get through difficult times. What happens when we are just not communicating well or getting along with our loved ones? Below are some suggested techniques to facilitate healthy communication and connection in your personal relationships, even when we are not functioning at our best.

The Relationship Tactical Disengagement. We all have our limits when it comes to how well we actively listen and effectively communicate throughout any given day. Factors such as sleep deprivation, emotions, mental or physical fatigue, stress, and hunger can impact how well we communicate. If you notice that you are unable to sustain communication or are preoccupied with other things, let your loved one know. Chances are that your brain and body will need some time to downshift from work mode. This is not a problem; however, you need to communicate that with your spouse. My husband and I learned this lesson the hard way. After years of bumping heads, we finally figured things out and came up with what we now call the "10-minute rule." If either of you recognizes that you need some time to decompress before engaging in conversation, simply say, "I need 10 minutes." This is code for, "Give me some physical space to decompress for a bit." It could take more or less than 10 minutes, so the exact amount of time does not necessarily matter. The point is that you are communicating what you need at that moment without making the other person feel invalidated or unwanted. If you feel that you need a bit more time (i.e., more than 20–30 minutes), do your best to frontload that information to your loved one ahead of time. For example, you can say something like, "It's been a difficult day. I'll need some time to decompress when I get home."

Take a Time-Out. When experiencing intense emotions, our communication suffers. Think about those moments when you have felt so angry, irritable, or annoyed that you spoke in a certain tone or were unable to listen because you were too busy formulating your response or trying hard to defend your position. This often happens because intense emotions hijack the brain's resources that are needed to actively listen and effectively communicate. This is where relationship damage can occur because we can say or do things that emotionally injure our partner. Establish a code word or phrase that you and your spouse use when emotions are highly charged and you recognize that a break is needed for either or both of you to cool down. The key here is to make sure that you *return* to the conversation. I've seen law enforcement couples "brush it off" or not bring the issue up again once the emotional intensity dissipates because they are worried about cycling up into another argument. Without correcting this behavior and properly healing the emotional injury, couples will inadvertently reinforce unhealthy communication and build resentment that can cause problems down the road.

Active Listening. Active listening is a simple, but not easy, skill to master. It involves being attentive, listening to the message beyond the words, and understanding (not necessarily agreeing) with the person's perspective or how they are feeling about something. A situation that upsets them or causes distress may be vastly different from the things you have experienced. That's okay. Remember that it is not a competition about who had the worst day or who deserves to feel a certain way. The goal is to *connect* with your loved one.

Much of the time, we humans just want to be heard and understood. If you are having difficulty understanding *why* your loved one is feeling or responding a certain way, shift your focus to connecting with the *feeling* they are verbalizing or conveying during that interaction. Are they feeling sad, angry, frustrated, anxious, or happy? Chances are that you've felt the same emotions at some point in your life. Although the circumstances may be different, sadness is sadness, anger is anger, anxiety is anxiety, and so on. Think about a time when you felt a similar emotion. How would you want your loved one to respond if you were feeling the same way? You would probably *not* want them to respond in a judgmental or dismissive manner. Instead, you'd likely want them to validate how you were feeling and convey support.

Help You or Hear You? When your loved one comes to

you with a problem, do your best to step out of your problem-solving role and actively listen to what they need. Do they need a sounding board? Do they need your help fixing the issue? The next time your loved one comes to you with an issue, it's okay to ask what they need. A helpful phrase is, "Do you need me to help you or hear you?" Their response will take out the guesswork and let you know what they need from you at that moment.

TRAIN UP FOR RETIREMENT

If you haven't done so already, begin training up your relationships to help you achieve a well-adjusted retired life. Take an honest look at your responses to the relationship questions you answered. What areas are going well? What areas need work? Talk with your loved ones and come up with a plan to address the problem areas and reinforce the good areas. I challenge you to begin using some of the above techniques to enhance your communication with loved ones. Keep in mind…this is an ongoing process that takes time and training to become proficient. Start working on this now if you haven't done so already.

If you run into roadblocks, talk with any friends/couples who seem to be doing well to identify what they are doing that you might want to implement in your own relationships. You can also do some online searching for additional information, books, or podcasts aimed at supporting healthy law enforcement relationships. If you are having difficulty getting started or need some additional tools, consider reaching out to a licensed counselor or psychologist who is trained in working with law enforcement couples and families.

CHAPTER 9
TRAINING UP FOR RETIREMENT

P reparing for retirement is a process that begins well before you sign on the dotted line. When it comes to having a well-adjusted retired life, *pre-retirement health, and functioning matter*. It is crucial to take inventory and to put the work in to reinforce your strengths and train up the areas that need some work. Retirement is not a magical fix for the issues that accumulate throughout your law enforcement career. Truth is, the grass is greener where you water it. Invest in yourself now so that you can have a fulfilling life after law enforcement. You gave so much to the job, and you deserve to squeeze every bit you can out of retirement.

WORKING THROUGH THE PHASES OF RETIREMENT

Just like you would debrief a call or situation you responded to at work, reflect on your responses to the questions posed throughout this book. What areas are going well? What areas can you improve upon? As you think about the four phases of retirement outlined in chapter one (Vacation, Feeling Loss and Lost, Trial and Error, and Reinvent and Rewire), what is going to help you through these phases, and what is going to hinder you? Set goals for growth leading up to and into retirement. What skills or additional resources do you need to bolster your ability to effectively work through the phases of retirement?

It is important to set non-work goals that focus on activities and relationships outside of the job. Consider any hobbies or other activities that you are open to learning or that you have let go over time because of job or family demands. It is also a good idea to incorporate activities or games designed to keep the mind sharp. Keep in mind that you are not the first cop to retire, nor will you be the last. Reach out to other law enforcement retirees about their experiences adjusting to retirement. What worked for them, and what didn't? Gather as much information as you can. This will help you interpret and navigate your own experiences when you get there.

YOU ARE MORE THAN A COP

Thriving in retirement involves embracing other aspects of your identity beyond being a cop. The job and its demands can easily overshadow other life roles, which can contribute to being overinvested at work and underinvested at home. When you reflect on your identity as a police officer, are you overinvested or healthy? What areas of life do you value outside of work? Are you doing things in service of these areas? Do your actions align with your values? If you find that you are a bit overinvested at work, set specific goals to broaden your identity in areas outside of work. Expanding your identity will help you find purpose and meaning beyond the badge. Not only will this help to mitigate job-related burnout and cynicism, but it will also set the stage for a healthy transition to retirement.

ACTIVELY WORK ON YOUR NEW ROUTINE

Actively restructuring your life in retirement is an important component of achieving a well-adjusted retired life. Think about what your new routine will look like in retirement. You do not need to have it all figured out but have a general sense of the basics. At a minimum, include some form of physical activity, interaction with others, and one activity that keeps your brain active. It also helps to begin identifying non-work enjoyable activities or hobbies that you can do to help you work through the Trial and Error phase of retirement.

One year prior to retirement, begin to get your brain and body used to a reduction in the level of daily stress and mental stimulation that accompanies the job. Reducing unnecessary overtime or taking an extra couple of days off work here and there can help. If you are able to reduce or eliminate paid overtime in the couple of years nearing retirement, that will help you adjust to the financial constraints of retirement. If you choose to work paid overtime, be sure to use that extra income to pay down debt or pad your savings account.

TAKE CARE OF YOUR PHYSICAL HEALTH

Physical health contributes to the quality of your retired life. Scheduling your annual physical exam with your medical provider helps to identify any health issues, formulate a treatment plan, and address any additional concerns or questions you have. Are there any weight loss or dietary goals that your provider can help you with? How about the quality of your sleep? Are there any lifestyle changes you can make to help address or prevent health issues?

If you have existing medical problems, are you receiving adequate treatment, and are your health needs being addressed? If not, take steps to get these needs met or find another medical provider if your current one is not a good fit. If you suffer from chronic pain or serious medical illness, how is your discomfort currently being addressed? Do you feel that you need to drink alcohol to help alleviate pain? Is your pain being effectively managed? Have you explored non-medication options to utilize in conjunction with your medical treatment?

If you receive medical treatment through workers' compensation benefits and plan to move out of state, be sure that you have a clear understanding of what these benefits will look like and the availability of workers' compensation medical providers in your new area.

KEEP NEGATIVITY AND CYNICISM IN CHECK

Your police training teaches you to adopt a distrustful attitude toward the intentions of others as a means of officer safety. Additionally, a career in law enforcement exposes you to the realities of all the bad that the world has to offer - violence, human depravity, tragic accidents, and betrayal by others. This is a recipe for adopting a negative and cynical mindset both on and off the job. Bringing this mindset into retirement can compromise your capacity to find purpose and fulfillment in life after law enforcement.

If you are a bit salty in the final stages of your career, work toward adopting realistic optimism. This is a balance between acknowledging the realities of life with a sprinkle of hope. In other words, consider the possibility of the good accompanying the bad. Cops tend to focus on and prepare for the worst. Truth is, not every situation ends up that way. Be sure to acknowledge the things that were not so bad the next time you encounter a problem, situation, or person. If your brain is thinking, "What if…" for something bad happening, also train your brain to think, "What if that doesn't happen?" or "What if something less bad happens?" This will help your brain build new connections for a healthier, more balanced mindset.

COPING WITH CHANGE

Think about how you cope with and adapt to change. Retirement equals change, and it is normal to feel a bit strange as you settle into retired life. The adjustment period can generally last from six months to two years. Are you going to embrace your humanness in retirement, or are you going to try to avoid it?

Remember that compartmentalizing emotions on duty is necessary to help you maintain objectivity and take decisive actions. Doing this off-duty can hinder your ability to connect with loved ones and inhibit your ability to tolerate emotional discomfort, which means you are more easily overwhelmed. Do you have difficulty sitting still or experience anxiety when your brain and body are not busy? Are you feeling irritable and angry off duty? If so, these are indicators that you may not be effectively coping with periods of discomfort. Be sure to train yourself to combat emotional avoidance when off duty and learn to stay engaged with discomfort and other emotions. What you resist, persists!

TAKE CARE OF YOUR MENTAL HEALTH

It is important to prioritize your mental health in retirement. Police work takes an inherent toll on your mental health, and it is normal to experience symptoms of depression, anxiety, and post-traumatic stress injuries at some point in your career and even into retirement. Without the distractions of work, the mental and emotional impact of the job can make an appearance. Pay attention to the impact of any symptoms you experience. If you need to seek additional tools and resources, do so.

HEALTHY RELATIONSHIPS

Healthy relationships have been shown to buffer against the stresses of life and the job. It takes a village to get through a law enforcement career, and the same applies to living well in retirement. The nature of police work poses some challenges to maintaining healthy relationships. It is not impossible, it just takes some additional work.

Your loved ones will be adjusting to your retirement just like they adjusted to your job. Communication is crucial to navigating those adjustments *together*. Identify your relationship strengths and challenges. Use the tools provided in this book to enhance communication. Seek out additional tools and resources when needed. Talk with your loved ones about retirement - what to expect, any fears or concerns, anything you are looking forward to, and the things you want to do.

FINDING PURPOSE AND FULFILLMENT BEYOND THE BADGE

Retirement marks the end of one chapter and the beginning of another. You now have the information and tools to write your retirement chapter with meaning and purpose. Preparing for retirement is an active and intentional process. Reinforce your strengths and enjoy the good times. Embrace any challenges you encounter as opportunities for growth. Take care of your body, your mind, and your relationships. Squeeze all the juice out of retirement!

AFTERWORD

FINAL THOUGHTS FROM ANTHONY BAUMGART, RETIRED POLICE OFFICER

My career lasted just over 29 years. I was hired as a patrol officer on my 21st birthday. I can remember thinking for the first ten years that I would have done this job for free. It was definitely for me, and I enjoyed it more than I can describe. Though that feeling of enjoying my career never went away, and I loved almost every minute of it, there is also a dark side. The side that gets to all of us eventually, turns us cynical and teaches most of us to hate people. This is one of the things that led to the timing of my retirement. Although my pension did not max for around eight more months, I pulled the pin. This is when I learned retirement is harder than it sounds. I would like to pass on a few things I learned. I know they are not the same for everyone, but this is from my perspective.

In my opinion, the actual goal of retirement is to be truly retired, which means not working. Many of us "retire" just to start a second job or career. I have lost count of how many people have told me they "have to" get another job because they can't afford to live on their pension. In California, the majority of departments max out their pension at thirty years with 90% of your gross salary. However, since many deductions end after retirement (pension, union dues, Medicare, etc.), your net pay retired is actually higher than when you worked, with the exception of the added overtime pay. Too many of us become dependent on overtime income. To counter this, I stopped taking overtime pay years before retirement and took comp time instead. This allowed me to relearn how to budget for my actual salary and not rely on overtime. It also allowed me to take off as much time as I wanted or needed near the end of my career.

I understand other states do not have as generous of a pension. Plus, everyone has their own financial burdens, and for some, not working may not be an option. Some people just want to work for various reasons having nothing to do with finances. For those people, I would suggest you try part-time work instead of another full-time job. Ask yourself how many people on their deathbed have said, "I wish I worked just one more day." Now ask yourself how many people on their deathbeds wished they had stopped working earlier. Many of us have friends that worked too long and died at their desks or shortly after retirement. Our days are limited whether we want them to be or not. Make the most of each and every one.

Other preparation is also needed…stuff no one thinks about until it hits. Not just for you but for your entire family. Are you married? Have kids? Your retirement will affect them as much as it does you. Everyone's daily routine is about to be blown up, and not everyone is going to adjust well or quickly. You should talk about these upcoming changes with any family members that still live with you. Learning to be retired, and trust me, it is a learning process, is not natural. I started working for friends or family at age thirteen, doing whatever I could and had a full-time job by sixteen. That was normal for our generation. Not working is unnatural to us. Most of us will go through trial and error before ending up happy in retirement. However, once you find that happy place, nothing will ever feel better. Every aspect of your life will improve - family, friends, health, happiness, etc.

While in the trial and error period and figuring out what your new routine will look like (routine is key), pay attention to what your family and friends are saying to you. These are the people that care about you the most and who will notice your changes for better or worse. If they start telling you they are concerned about something in your life (drinking too much, obvious depression or anger, etc.), don't ignore their concerns or blame them for not understanding. My wife was the one that had concerns about some of the things I was doing, and as painful as it is to say these words, she was 100% right. Things did not improve until I changed what I was doing and how I approached retired life.

Remind yourselves that if you had to work for 25-30 years in your career to get to where you are, your new goal needs to be enjoying your retirement for another 25-30 years. To drive home that point, you paid money into your retirement system your entire career. During your first twelve to fifteen years of retirement, you are basically getting paid back the money you gave them. Until that money runs out, you have not earned anything from your pension. For me, the magic number is 12 1/2 years. Once I have been retired for twelve years and seven months, I will finally be drawing money from the pension system and not just getting my own money back. I have every intention of taking as much of their money as possible. All of you should feel the same way.

People ask me what I notice the most now that I have been retired for over six years. My answer is always the same. Before I retired, I was angry all the time, and I hated people. Now, I am seldom angry, but I still hate people. The reality, though, is I also am always happy, never stressed out, healthier, and love my life and my family. I wish all of you the same.

ADDITIONAL RESOURCES

The below resources are helpful should you want additional information or need additional support. This is not an exhaustive list.

Bulletproof Spirit (book), by Dan Willis
Police Captain Dan Willis offers field-tested expertise designed to be used by first responders and their families to heal themselves and continue serving with compassion and strength.

Change Your Brain, Change Your Pain (book), by Mark Grant
This book describes the role of the brain in human experience, the relationship between the brain and the body, and why it's important to understand how your brain works when you are dealing with chronic pain. After learning how the effects of stress on the brain impact pain, the author provides several self-help strategies designed to reverse the patterns of brain activity that maintain pain.

Purchase of the book provides access to audio downloads of exercises.

Code 4 Couples – www.code4couples.com

Founded by Cyndi Doyle, a licensed counselor and police wife, Code4Couples offers a wealth of information on law enforcement relationships. Her podcast also discusses issues relevant to law enforcement spouses and couples, including retirement.

Cop Line – www.copline.org or (800) 267-5463

A not-for-profit organization dedicated to serving law enforcement officers by providing 24/7 trained peer support for anything ranging from a bad day to a crisis. They offer referrals to skilled mental health professionals for follow-up and continued assistance. Cop Line is a confidential hotline answered by retired law enforcement officers who have access to continuous clinical support. This is also a great organization to volunteer for when you retire if interested. Their website provides additional information regarding training for all volunteers.

Emotional Survival for Law Enforcement (book), by Kevin M. Gilmartin

This book is essential for all police officers. It highlights the behavioral, attitude, and physical changes that occur in someone through the course of police work. Dr. Gilmartin's website is www.emotionalsurvival.com, and offers additional information and resources.

Hold the Line (book), by Cyndi Doyle

Cyndi is a licensed professional counselor and the wife

of a police officer. Her book addresses the impact of the job on both the officer and spouse, psychology behind the cop brain and its effects on behavior and beliefs, spillover that may impact the spouse and family, conflict in law enforcement relationships, and strategies to foster a healthy relationship with your spouse.

Increasing Resilience in Police and Emergency Personnel: Strengthening Your Mental Armor (book), by Stephanie M. Conn, www.firstresponderpsychology.com

Dr. Conn is a former police officer and a psychologist who is dedicated to enhancing the resilience of first responders. This book highlights the psychological, emotional, behavioral, and spiritual impact of police work on officers, administrators, emergency communicators, and their families. She debunks myths about weakness and offers practical strategies in plain language for police employees and their families struggling with traumatic stress and burnout. She provides strengths-based guidance to help navigate the many complex and sometimes difficult effects of police and emergency work.

National Law Enforcement Cancer Support Foundation, www.lawenforcementcancer.org

This organization provides free emotional support, guidance, and resources to members of the law enforcement community (active and retired) during a cancer experience.

National Suicide and Crisis Lifeline – www.988lifeline.org or call/text 988

This hotline provides 24/7, free and confidential

support, for people in suicidal crisis or emotional distress, as well as prevention and crisis resources for you or your loved ones.

Relentless Courage (book), by Michael Sugrue and Shauna Springer

This book offers a firsthand account of the toll of first responder trauma and offers insights by a police psychologist to help first responders make sense of experiences they may encounter over the course of their career.

Behind the Badge: 365 Daily Devotions for Law Enforcement, by Adam Davis

This book is written by former law enforcement officer Adam Davis and is a #1 bestseller for law enforcement. To learn more, visit www.TheAdamDavis.com.

Safe Call Now – www.safecallnow.org or (206) 459-3020

Safe Call Now is a confidential, comprehensive 24/7 crisis referral service for all public safety employees, all emergency services personnel, and their family members nationwide.

Wounded Blue – www.thewoundedblue.org or (877) 810-0911

This organization's mission is to improve the lives of injured and disabled law enforcement officers (active and retired) through support, education, assistance, and legislation.

ABOUT THE AUTHOR

Dr. Medina Baumgart is a licensed psychologist and Board Certified in Police and Public Safety Psychology by the American Board of Professional Psychology. She has extensive experience working with sworn and civilian law enforcement personnel in both correctional and law enforcement agency settings. Dr. Baumgart is married to a now-retired police officer and understands firsthand the challenges that some cops face transitioning to retired life. She and her husband share their personal and professional experiences with other police officers and spouses in their *Surviving Retirement* training class. Dr. Baumgart continues to share her expertise with law enforcement officers, retirees, spouses, and agencies through presentations on a wide range of wellness topics that are informed by her experience, research, and clinical practice.

NOTES

1. UNDERSTANDING RETIREMENT

1. Wang, M. & Hesketh, B. (2012). *Achieving well-being in retirement: Recommendations from 20 years of research.* Society for Industrial and Organizational Psychology, Inc.
2. Wang, M. & Hesketh, B. (2012). *Achieving well-being in retirement: Recommendations from 20 years of research.* Society for Industrial and Organizational Psychology, Inc.
3. Violanti, J.M. (1992) *Police Retirement: The impact of change.* Springfield, Illinois: Thomas.
4. Violanti, J.M. (1992) *Police Retirement: The impact of change.* Springfield, Illinois: Thomas.
5. Adapted from "Annual Check-In" by Dr. Stephanie M. Conn and shared with her permission, First Responder Psychology, www.firstresponderpsychology.com
6. Dr. Riley Moynes: 4 Phases of Retirement…and the Psychological Challenges. TED Talk. https://www.ted.com/talks/dr_riley_moynes_the_4_phases_of_retirement

2. I GAVE YOU MY LIFE, AND YOU HANDED ME A RECEIPT

1. Conti, N. (2009). A Visigoth system: Shame, honor, and police socialization. *Journal of Contemporary Ethnography, 38(3),* 409-432.
2. Reitzes, D.C., & Mutran, E.J. (2004). The transition into retirement: Stages and factors that influence retirement adjustment. *International Journal of Aging and Human Development, 59,* 63-84.
3. Adapted from the book, *Bouncing back from trauma: The essential step-by-step guide for police readiness,* by Frank J. Gallo, Ph.D.
4. Thoits, P.A. (2013). Self, Identity, Stress, and Mental Health. In: Aneshensel, C.S., Phelan, J.C., Bierman, A. (eds) Handbook of the Sociology of Mental Health. Handbooks of Sociology and Social Research. Springer, Dordrecht. https://doi.org/10.1007/978-94-007-4276-5_18

4. PHYSICAL WEAR AND TEAR

1. Violanti, J.M., Vena, J.E., & Petralia, S. (1998). Mortality of a police cohort: 1950-1990. *American Journal of Industrial Medicine, 33*, 366-373.
2. Ramey, S.L., Downing, N.R., & Knoblauch (2008). Developing strategic interventions to reduce cardiovascular disease risk among law enforcement officers: the art and science of data triangulation. *AAOHNJ, 56*, 54-62.
3. Violanti, J.M. (Ed.) (2014). *Dying for the job: Police work exposure and health.* Charles C Thomas Publisher: Springfield, Illinois.

7. MENTAL AND EMOTIONAL IMPACT

1. Conn, S.M. (2018). *Increasing resilience in police and emergency personnel: Strengthening your mental armor,* Routledge: NY.
2. Gershon, R. M., Barocas, B., Canton, A., Li, X., & Vlahov, D. (2009). Mental, physical, and behavioral outcomes associated with perceived work stress in police officers. *Criminal Justice and Behavior, 36*(3), 275-289.
3. Paton, D. & Norris, K. (2014). Vulnerability to work-related posttraumatic stress (chapter). In John Violanti's (editor) book *Dying for the Job,* Charles C. Thomas Publisher: Springfield, Illinois.
4. Personal communication (4/11/23). Dr. Mariya Dvoskina and Dr. John Nicoletti. Shared with permission.